Systems Analysis

WITHDRAWN STOCK.

Systems Analysis

A Beginner's Guide

Kevin Bowman
Sheffield Hallam University

palgrave
macmillan

First published 2004 by
PALGRAVE MACMILLAN
Houndmills, Basingstoke, Hampshire RG21 6XS and
175 Fifth Avenue, New York, N. Y. 10010
Companies and representatives throughout the world

PALGRAVE MACMILLAN is the global academic imprint of the Palgrave Macmillan division of St. Martin's Press, LLC and of Palgrave Macmillan Ltd. Macmillan® is a registered trademark in the United States, United Kingdom and other countries. Palgrave is a registered trademark in the European Union and other countries.

ISBN 978-0-333-98630-1 (pbk)
ISBN 978-0-333-98630-1   ISBN 978-0-230-00568-6 (eBook)
DOI 10.1007/978-0-230-00568-6

This book is printed on paper suitable for recycling and made from fully managed and sustained forest sources. Logging, pulping and manufacturing processes are expected to conform to the environmental regulations of the country of origin.

A catalogue record for this book is available from the British Library.

10   9   8   7   6   5   4   3   2   1
13 12 11 10 09 08 07 06 05 04

To Mum and Dad

Contents

Preface

This book teaches the key techniques used in SSADM and is an ideal starting text for first-year undergraduate computing students or those at Foundation or HND level. It is not intended to be an SSADM manual; instead, it strips SSADM down to the key techniques and explains these in simple terms without the common repetition and over-elaboration found in other books in this area. Most real-world systems use such a cut-down version, and this book provides the reader with a sound awareness of the fundamental skills required for successful systems analysis and design.

The book uses a step-by-step approach, assuming no previous knowledge and avoiding jargon. Chapter 1 provides an overview of systems analysis, and Chapter 2 goes on to introduce the approach of this book and the two case studies that will develop throughout the text. Chapters 3–8 then detail each key stage in systems analysis and design. A complete teaching case study is provided in the Appendix.

The book contains an abundance of examples, end of chapter exercises, and two case studies: the Swillbuckets Country Club and the Medical Centre at the University of Life. The use of humour is central and the case studies have been designed to give ample opportunity to make the text amusing while demonstrating the key points. The book is also accompanied by a dedicated lecturer and student web site which features solutions to all the exercises and working versions of the case studies.

Acknowledgements

Special thanks to Liz for support and giving me precious time. Thanks to Danny, Holly, Tom and Jack for giving me the incentive. Someone's got to pay those university fees.

Thanks also to Steve Wade for the inspiration.

CHAPTER 1

Introduction to systems analysis

1.1 ▍ What is a system?

It is sometimes assumed that a system always refers to a computer system, but of course there are many other types of system. The human body, for example, is a complex system made up of many smaller systems: the respiratory system, the digestive system etc.

We could loosely define a system as anything with a purpose. A system must do something. If you put something into it, you should get something different out of it. So this book is a system for learning about systems analysis. If you input the time and effort required to read it, as indeed you are doing, you will gain unparalleled insights into systems analysis techniques, Swillbuckets Club, normalization and all manner of joys.

But nearly everything has a purpose. It's hard to think of something that has no purpose. Morning television, perhaps. Or museum attendants, maybe. Generally, though, we could take the view that everything is a system.

It certainly seems to be true that every system is made up of smaller systems, and also that every system is part of a larger system. The college or university you attend is a system, though it might not always seem like it. It is made up of departments, classes and students, all of which are systems themselves. Expanding upwards, the college or university is a part of the education system of the country, which in turn is part of the public services, and so on.

Sometimes, it's hard to know when one system stops and another one starts. The systems analyst has to make this decision early on: exactly what is the scope of the system being analysed? Otherwise, the analyst could be analysing away for ever.

1.2 | Information systems

Most, if not all, organizations have an information system. It might be quite primitive, like a list of names and addresses stuffed into a shoebox, or it might be hugely sophisticated. Either way, the aims will be pretty much the same: to help provide an effective customer service and to help management make the best decisions.

In order to understand how information systems can help organizations, you need to understand the difference between data and information. Data is raw facts or figures such as: 42, 12, 45, 13, 9 and 34. These numbers have no meaning until you know the context. They might be lottery numbers, map coordinates or a secret code. They need to be processed in some way to turn them into something useful. When this has been done, you have information.

Information is useful to somebody. It tells you something you didn't know before. Sometimes it's not that important and can be ignored; sometimes it's priceless. How much would advance information about the September 11th 2001 terrorist attacks have been worth? Of course, information systems in businesses won't provide that type of information, but they might make the difference between success and failure. Figure 1.1 shows how information systems work in essence.

Figure 1.1
Information systems.

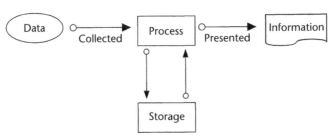

The raw data needs to be processed in some way to produce information. The data might be sorted into alphabetical order. Or key elements of the data might be filtered out. Or the data might just be presented in a more understandable way. It's your job as the systems analyst, in conjunction with the user, to decide what processing of data takes place and how it happens.

1.3 | What is systems analysis?

There's a lot more to building an information system than sitting down at a PC and starting to type. In the past, before systems analysis existed, programmers went into organizations, spoke to a couple of senior managers, went away and came back a few months later with a new system. But this wasn't a very successful approach. It assumed that users knew what system they wanted. That's like an aeroplane engine manufacturer asking passengers what sort of engine they want. They just want one that works!

Equally, users of computer systems usually don't know what sort of system they want; they just want one that works. Some of them don't even want a new system. They just know that there are a few problems here and there.

So the job of the systems analyst is to find out what is good and what is bad about the system they currently have, and then design a new system that keeps the good things and gets rid of the bad things. Sounds simple, but it's not.

To begin with, there are always gaps between the user and the systems analyst. The user understands the current system, but the analyst doesn't. The analyst understands the new system, but the user doesn't. How well the analyst and user work together to bridge these gaps will determine how successful the new system is.

Effective communication between user and analyst is therefore vital. The analyst must involve the user in all stages of the systems analysis process. This will help bridge the gaps. But how will the user understand the complexities of systems analysis? After all, the user might not know much more about computers than how to type a memo or play golf.

That's one problem. Here's another. Can you believe what users tell you? Alice in Sales might have all kinds of reasons for telling you that she needs a new interactive, web-enabled, real-time, dynamic Orders system, but the real problem might be that nobody wants to buy their products.

Then again, Alice's boss might have a very different view of what an Orders system should look like (and cost!). There might be lots of 'politics' going on which causes requirements to change. The systems analyst needs a method of avoiding these pitfalls. This brings us on to methodologies.

1.4 Systems Methodologies

The other thing to be aware of about systems is that they are all very complicated. Usually, they are too complicated for anyone to understand without tools and techniques to help them. This is where methodologies come in. They're there to help. If they don't help, there's no point in bothering with them.

A methodology is a strategy for overcoming the problems faced by the systems analyst. It's made up of techniques, tools, conventions and documents, and it lays down the tasks to be done.

It's like cooking a meal. If you follow the recipe, you might end up with something edible. If you make it up as you go along, you usually end up with a brown mess.

One type of methodology is called *structured*. Structured methodologies are very popular with systems analysts. They are just like recipes for building computer systems. They lay down steps that the analyst should follow in a clear order. If the analyst follows these steps, then eventually a quality information systems design should be the outcome. Structured methodologies also allow the analyst to break down complex systems into smaller, well-defined and well-documented chunks.

The most widely used structured methodology is SSADM.

1.5 | SSADM – Structured Systems Analysis and Design Method

SSADM contains in it some basic principles that should help overcome the problems we've mentioned:

1 The first principle is the one just mentioned, about breaking down complex systems into chunks. This is called top down functional decomposition. It means that the analyst starts off just thinking about the system as a whole. Small details are ignored to begin with until the analyst has a grasp of the key features of the system. Later on, the analyst will think about the more detailed lower levels of the system.

2 The scope of SSADM is clearly defined. The analyst starts off by looking at the physical aspects of the current system. This means looking at *how* things are currently done and *who* does them. The analyst then moves on to look at *what* is currently done from a logical point of view. This completes the analysis phase, and then it's on to design. The analyst will consider what the new system should do and finally how it should do it. This is as far as SSADM goes. This approach might be represented as in Figure 1.2.

Figure 1.2
SSADM approach.

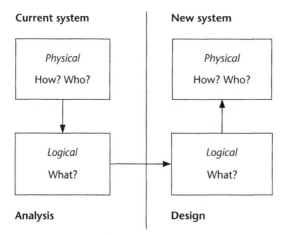

3 SSADM requires users to get involved from the start. This makes them more committed to the process and more likely to be happy with the new system. The analyst must meet the users regularly to sort out problems and check understanding. Incidentally, this means that the analyst should possess highly developed communication skills. These are possibly the most important skills of all in systems analysis.

4 SSADM makes effective use of diagrams to help both the analyst and the user understand the system. These diagrams should be simple and easy to follow, like a map of the system.

5 SSADM allows the analyst to see the system from different views. You can then check to see if the different views match up. This is called cross-checking.

6 SSADM has been around for a good many years. It's an industry standard, so most analysts have used it. If your life depended on a system being successful, you might well use SSADM as the best bet to save your skin.

1.6 The structure of SSADM

SSADM is made up of a number of Stages. These Stages are then divided up into Steps. Figure 1.3 shows an overview of the Stages.

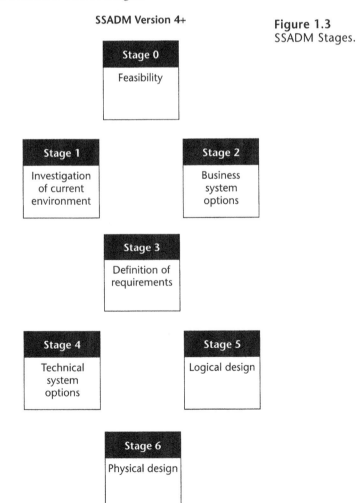

SSADM Version 4+

Figure 1.3
SSADM Stages.

Stage 0: Feasibility

This is where the analyst and users decide if the entire project is worth pursuing. It involves the analyst considering the problems faced by the organization and producing a set of options to resolve them. The users must then decide whether the costs involved in resolving the problem are worth it. It may be that the problems are so severe that the organization simply has to resolve them. In this case, the feasibility study might be left out.

Stage 1: Investigation of the current environment

This needs to be done so that the analyst and the users fully understand what the current system does. They need to be clear what problems they have and what they want from the new system.

Stage 2: Business system options

This Stage allows the analyst and users to come up with some ideas about what the new system might do. Usually, a range of options, with different costs and benefits, are considered. Users will need to be clear about the objectives of the business before they can choose the option to proceed with.

Stage 3: Definition of requirements

This involves specifying the required system. During this Stage, the analyst will want to move away from the constraints of the current system and towards a more logical, data-driven design. An overview of the underlying data structures for the required system is created.

Stage 4: Selection of technical system options

By now, the analyst and users will have a reasonable idea of what the new system will be expected to do. This allows them to consider the technical options. For example, the key hardware components will need to be identified and costed. The users will, eventually, choose from a range of options.

Stage 5: Logical design

This involves specifying the new system. What will the new system do? What might it look like from a user perspective?

Stage 6: Physical design

This Stage concentrates on the environment within which the new system will be running. It involves looking at storage requirements and performance issues.

At the end of each of these Stages, the analyst and users must decide whether to press on to the next Stage, abandon the project, or redo one or more Stages. All of these cost money.

1.7 ▌ SSADM and the Systems Development Life Cycle

SSADM isn't the end of the story – it's just part of it. The whole process of systems development goes further still. SSADM stops with the design of the new system, but systems development goes on. Most projects go through the stages outlined in Figure 1.4. This is the Systems Development Life Cycle.

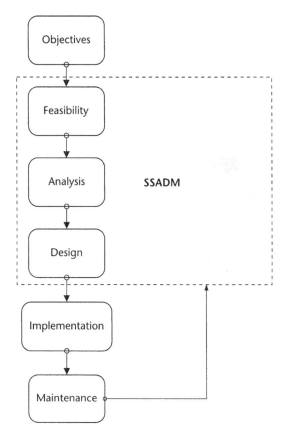

Figure 1.4
The Systems Development Life Cycle.

   However, even this may not be the end of the process, as organizations change and it may soon be time to start the whole process again.

Summary

We have described what systems analysis is and the need for a methodology to help the analyst. We have described the most popular methodology – SSADM – and considered its advantages and how it fits into the Systems Development Life Cycle.

Exercises

1.1 What functions does the systems analyst perform during the Systems Development Life Cycle (SDLC)?

1.2 The SDLC is just one model for systems development. Find at least one more and describe the differences.

1.3 Why has SSADM become an industry standard?

CHAPTER 2

The current system

2.1 ▎ The approach in this book

It is not the approach of this book to go through each SSADM Stage and Step in detail. Rather, the book focuses on the key techniques used at each Stage and applies them to a case study or two. Each technique will be explained in simple steps using the case studies as examples.

The approach is to present a cut-down version of SSADM. This version has all the techniques and steps necessary for a successful systems analysis and design, but cuts out some of the repetition and over elaboration. Most real-world systems analysts use such a cut-down version.

2.2 ▎ The case studies

There are two main case studies in this book. They are central to the book and should be read carefully. The case studies concern the Swillbuckets Country Club and the Medical Centre at the University of Life.

2.2.1 Swillbuckets Country Club

General

Swillbuckets Country Club is a club for the people of West Yorkshire. Each weekend, the members roll up eager for refreshment and keenly anticipating the entertainment booked by Jack Trout, the Swillbuckets Secretary. Some of the more popular acts include 'Chucky Egg the Chicken Hypnotist', 'Sharon Twain Entertains' and 'Jade Green and her Dancing Chihuahuas'.

Jack has a number of tasks to perform at Swillbuckets. As well as booking the artistes, he also has to enrol new members, produce payslips to pay the acts, advertise future events and chase up subscriptions. He also prides himself on his choice of meat dishes at the events, though the chef, Freddo Smith, should take some credit. Not much, though.

The problem background

Jack has always used a card-based data storage system to keep information about members and artistes – essentially two or three shoeboxes full of dog-eared cards. Given the current popularity of Swillbuckets, this shoebox system (SS) is no longer adequate. Jack has the option of opening up yet more shoeboxes or going computerized. These are the issues he is grappling with.

A key problem that Jack is currently encountering revolves around members' subscriptions. Amanda Stote (Assistant Subscriptions Supervisor – ASS) helps Jack collect the subscriptions. Amanda is not a patient person. She asked Jack two weeks ago for a list of all the members with overdue subscriptions. Jack has been unable to provide it, since it entails working through the entire shoebox, checking all the expiry dates of members' subscriptions and then writing out the list.

A second headache for Jack has been amending members' records. He has favoured the White Fluid Approach To Amendment (WFATA). But the problems are legion: applying the correction fluid, making a drink while it dries, forgetting to make the correction etc.

Jack also produces a monthly Forthcoming Events list, which he sends off to local media such as *Farm to Table News* and *Trucks and Tractors*.

Jack prides himself on the imaginative range of foodstuffs available at Swillbuckets. Jack is a connoisseur of meat, or, more specifically, offal. He likes nothing better than tucking in to a sweetmeat or two of an afternoon. But the catering side of things is a real problem. Jack acquires his meat through a variety of suppliers. One of his main suppliers, Tommy Chillmore, often turns up round the back of the club with a bag of skinned rabbits, or ducks. You never quite know what you're going to get with Tommy. Jack has to negotiate a price using techniques such as pointing out that poaching is illegal. He pays Tommy in cash and stuffs the 'fresh produce' in the freezer. None of this is ever recorded. The result is that Jack has no real idea what is in stock at any given time.

This makes life difficult for Freddo Smitho, the chef. He comes in with a recipe in mind, specifically targeting the clientele for that evening's event. For example, when Gypsy Ky-Lee performs, scrag end of mutton hash seems to be the meal of choice. Imagine Freddo's horror when he discovers that Jack has not ordered any mutton, but has a pigeon mountain instead. Often the menu has to be rewritten at the last minute.

Fortunately, some suppliers are more reliable and prefer to do things by the book. The local brewery, Cooper's, is particularly diligent when it comes to paperwork and deliveries are always punctual. However, Jack gets confused when trying to operate proper business arrangements with some suppliers and a more relaxed approach to legal requirements with others.

2.2.2 The Medical Centre at the University of Life

General

The Medical Centre caters mainly for students and staff at the University of Life. Registration takes place each year when new students take their enrolment numbers to the Centre and register as patients. The University sends the Medical Centre a list of all students enrolled each year so that they can double check that a prospective patient is enrolled.

It is also possible for local residents to enrol if they live within the catchment area and if there is room on a doctor's list.

Once a patient is enrolled, the Medical Centre sends details to the General Practitioners' Council (GPC). The GPC will then issue a new Medical Card directly to the patient. If a patient leaves the Centre, the GPC must be informed. The GPC will fund the Centre and pay salaries depending upon the number of patients enrolled.

Patients can attempt to make an appointment at the Centre, though usually their condition will have cleared up by the time the appointment occurs. Patients must then cancel their appointments or be open to public ridicule. A 'name and shame' list of patients who forgot to cancel appointments is on display in the waiting room. If they do get to see a doctor, they will be prescribed paracetamol or penicillin. This works fine in most cases, but the head lice epidemic shows no sign of abating.

In the rare cases where the doctors admit defeat, they will refer patients (if still breathing) to the local hospital. Alternatively, they might ask for a second opinion. However, this will rarely be useful as they will already have tried paracetamol.

Staff

There are four doctors and a nurse. The nurse, Constance Payne, deals mainly with vaccinations and repeat prescriptions. She is also responsible for ordering supplies when they get low. Supplies might be anything from plasters to syringes.

Each doctor has a list of patients for whom he or she is the GP. However, it is possible for patients to see other doctors if their own doctor is not on duty.

There are two receptionists, George and Betty, and a trainee receptionist, Chelsea, who are responsible for dealing with patient queries and maintaining the Appointments Book. This is a very hit and miss affair, as the following transcript shows:

Reception

George: I've got a girl on the phone, Betty. She wants to go on Doctor Spock's list.

Betty: We haven't got a Doctor Spock, George. He was on the telly, funny ears, from outer space I think dear.

George: That's what I told her, she must mean Doctor Spackman.

Betty: Ask her where she lives.

George: 47 Thomson Road.

Betty: Never heard of it. Where's the street map?

George: Chelsea had it when she was looking for that boy's address, Dean was it?

Betty: Oh yes, didn't exist though did it. Shame for her. Still, she'll learn. Where is Chelsea?

George: Eh?

Betty: Where's Chelsea?

George: London, I think.

Betty: Really? What's she doing there? Has that Dean upset her again?

George: No that was last week. I'll put her on Dr McLean's list. He's a bit low, what with the court case and the flu jab mix-up.

Betty: What's this say in the Appointment Book? Mr Enkab Rolow?

George: Looks like Nek Bralow to me.

Betty: Hold on, this name's been crossed out. There's another one squashed underneath – Conquest. That's it Norman Conquest – daft name. Eh, George, look at this, Norman Conquest. Oh, hello Mr Conquest. Looks like you and Mr Bralow have got the same appointment. Would you mind waiting? You too Mrs Stote? Well I'm sure Dr. McLean will be here soon. Just take a seat. George, Mrs Stote's records: where are they? She's not even down for an appointment but I daren't tell her. She put the butcher in hospital when he told her he had no trotters and would ribs do?

George: Don't worry Betty love, I'm sure they're here somewhere. I remember seeing them. The cat had hold of them... where is it? Under the stairs, I think.

Betty: Mrs Stote's records under the stairs!

George: No the cat. I think Dr McLean had Mrs Stote's records, or was that the cat? I can't remember. I can't remember anything these days. Where am I?

Betty: Here they are, under the street map.

George: The street map. Didn't I want that? There's a girl still on the phone. Where's the phone gone?

Problem background

The problem areas can be summed up as:

- **Appointments**: chaotic, with double bookings, no room for urgent cases, and changes not made. A foolproof system of appointments is the top priority for the Centre.

- **Patient processing**: the filing of records is haphazard. They can go missing, or be misfiled. With such a high turnover of patients, the records are not always maintained accurately. Much information is duplicated and often disparities appear. The doctors require a way of viewing patient records without having to keep going backwards and forwards to see Betty and George. Prescriptions are normally illegible, which results in Heather in the chemists having to pop in regularly to have them decrypted.

- **management information**: the GPC requires regular information about the hours doctors have worked, new patients, supplies used etc. Currently, Nurse Payne attempts to produce these, but mathematics is not her strong point. The staff time sheets are a mess and staff often get paid for hours they haven't worked. The accountant is not happy about this. Neither is the GPC.

  The GPC also needs regular updates on currently enrolled patients. It is the responsibility of the receptionists to record when patients leave and keep a list of patients for each doctor. However, the University does not tell them when a student withdraws, and patients rarely think to inform them when they move away. The only information it gets is from the GPC when it issues a new Medical Card for another practice, or from the Registrar of Deaths. Betty gets quite queasy when she has to tear up someone's medical records and throw them in the bin.

  The Prescription Monitoring Agency also requires information about what prescriptions have been issued so that it can compare different practices and see who is out of line. It sends a report every six months to the Centre. This is shredded and used as a home for the hamster.

  The accountant requires regular financial information about outgoings. This is the bane of Nurse Payne's life. A proper accounting system is required.

- **Ordering supplies**: on a more mundane note, Nurse Payne has no information about potential suppliers, other than the catalogues she keeps under her desk. She may be paying too much for bandages etc. She is keen to find out more about some recycled Crimean War bandages that her friend, Nurse Blunt mentioned to her.

- **Registration**: it has been known for the receptionists to take down details wrongly (e.g. 'blood group'), or to omit key words such as 'haemophiliac'. These typing errors have had unnerving results. Also, George and Betty have had problems trying to determine who is eligible to join the practice. A street map with felt tip lines on it has proven to be a less than adequate tool. Ideally, they want to be able to say instantly if a postcode is within their catchment area.

The remainder of this chapter will consist of an analysis of the two case studies using structured systems analysis techniques. This chapter will focus on the Medical Centre, though there will be some examples from Swillbuckets also. We will assume that the feasibility study (Stage 0) has given us the green light to go ahead. We are about to start Stage 1: Investigation of the Current Environment, as shown in Figure 2.1.

Figure 2.1
SSADM Stage 1.

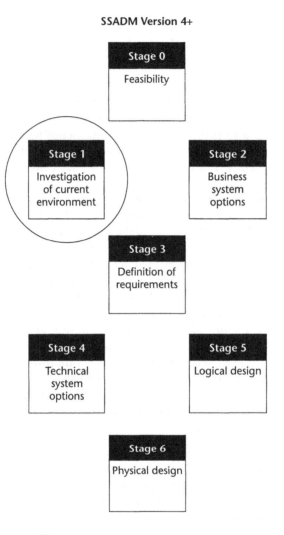

SSADM Version 4+

Stage 0

Feasibility

Stage 1

Investigation of current environment

Stage 2

Business system options

Stage 3

Definition of requirements

Stage 4

Technical system options

Stage 5

Logical design

Stage 6

Physical design

2.3 ▌ Investigation of the current environment

Remember that we are investigating the current environment so that we can identify problems, record requirements and generally understand what the organization does. We will focus on the Steps needed to accomplish this. Not all of the formal SSADM Steps will be covered.

2.3.1 Investigate and define requirements

As we work through the analysis of the current system, we need to be teasing out problems and requirements. Sometimes, these will be thrust in the analyst's face. On other occasions, they will be well hidden and only appear when it's too late. All these problems and requirements need to be written down in the Requirements Catalogue. The Requirements Catalogue might consist of a collection of forms like the blank one shown in Figure 2.2.

Problems/requirements catalogue	

Figure 2.2
Requirements
Catalogue.

System:		
Author:		
Date:	Page of	Draft/final

P/R	No:	Source:	Priority:

Description:
Benefits if action taken:
Comments/suggested solutions:
Related probs/reqts/documents:

If we were to consider the Medical Centre case study, the first entry in our Requirements Catalogue might look like the one in Figure 2.3.

The P/R option requires the analyst to enter whether this is a problem (P) or a requirement (R). The Priority section requires a quick decision to be made on the priority of the requirement. It may be that only the top priorities can be implemented, for example. Normally, these range from top priority (1) to low priority (5).

The final section allows the analyst to link together problems and requirements, if appropriate. So the problem in Figure 2.3 might well be linked to a requirement to introduce a computerized appointments system which prevents double booking.

Typical problems that the analyst might look for are:

● The current system is unreliable in some way.

● The current system lacks integrity: it can't be trusted to give accurate information.

Figure 2.3
Requirements
Catalogue entry.

Problems/requirements catalogue

System: Medical Centre		
Author: Kevin Bowman		
Date: 30/10/03	Page 1 of 1	Draft/~~final~~

P/R P	No: 1	Source: Betty	Priority: 1

Description:
Double booking is occurring as a result of the Appointments Book being hard to maintain accurately.

Benefits if action taken:
No more arguments with Amanda Stote. Patients seen on time. Fewer complaints.

Comments/suggested solutions:
Computerised Appointments Data Entry Form to include Patients combo box and pre-formatted appointment slots.

Related probs/reqts/documents:
Requirement 1
DFD Appointments

- The current system is easy to break into.
- The current system has no proper backup procedures in place.
- The current system does not perform adequately at peak times.
- The current system cannot be adapted to meet current and future needs.

Improvements in these areas might well be requirements of the new system.

2.3.2 Fact-finding techniques

It is worth considering what the best ways are for getting information about the system from users. Interviews are the main technique, but the analyst has to be well prepared for these. It is no use turning up with a blank piece of paper and no plan. The analyst should set up interviews with one person at a time, at a specific time and date. The time and date must be at the user's convenience. It is normally best to start with top management, as they have more of an overview of the organization.

It is very difficult to follow what someone is saying about their role in a system when you are trying to write notes at the same time. It is much easier to record the interview and listen to it later, as long as the interviewee doesn't mind. This allows the analyst to think about the user's comments and pursue different lines of enquiry more effectively.

It is preferable to have a few key questions prepared in advance, though it is important that users are allowed to talk about what is important to them.

The analyst must be careful not to create conflict and mistrust by discussing with users what other users have said. Similarly, the analyst must not prejudge the issue and tell users what sort of system they might be getting. Interviewing users is a difficult skill, acquired mainly by experience. Beginners should keep it simple and not be afraid to go back for clarification.

It is also useful to be able to consider the current system by looking at the existing paperwork. This can give many insights into the problems of the current system, as well as indicating what data flows around the system. Forms and files have the advantage of being unbiased and they do not harbour grievances against colleagues – unlike users.

So, grab as many forms, files and scraps of paper as you possibly can on your visits to the organization – with the users' agreement, of course.

2.3.3 Investigate current processing

This Step also involves fact-finding, but focuses on producing models or diagrams of the processing in the current system. The key technique here is Data Flow Modelling.

Data Flow Modelling
Data Flow Modelling allows the analyst to get a picture of the current system and think about the required system. It involves producing a number of diagrams which show how the current system works and what the required system might do. Figure 2.4 models this process.

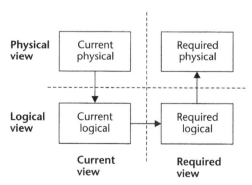

Figure 2.4
Data modelling in SSADM.

At this stage of SSADM, the diagrams include: context diagrams, document flow diagrams and Data Flow Diagrams (DFDs). Of these, DFDs are the most important, so we'll start with those.

Data flow diagrams

Data flow diagrams are central to SSADM. They show the processes involved in the current (and required) system, what data is involved, and where the data goes to. DFDs are about processes, primarily things that are done – activities. If someone asked you to list the activities involved in, say, getting out of the house in a morning, you might produce these: getting out of bed, washing, shaving (optional), getting dressed, eating breakfast, checking the time, leaving the house. Notice that these all contain verbs, because they are activities. If you put this list into the form of a diagram, you might end up with something like Figure 2.5.

Figure 2.5
Morning activities.

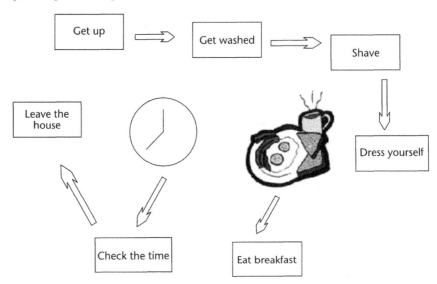

This has much in common with a DFD. It includes the activities and any data which is needed to perform the activities. For example, the correct time is needed in order to know when to 'leave the house'. This kind of data flow, into and out of activities, is very common in DFDs. So DFDs are nothing to fear: they are a tool to help the analyst understand the system.

DFDs show how information is created, altered or moved around by the system. They also show how it is received into the system and stored.

Data flow diagram conventions

There are four elements to a DFD. These are:

● Processes (or activities)

● Data flows

● External entities

● Data stores

Processes

The processes show an activity carried out by someone in the organization which involves data in some way. They take the form of a box with the activity inside. The activity always starts with a verb, such as 'Pay artistes' at Swillbuckets. The processes are numbered in the top left-hand corner. This is just to identify the process: it does not mean that process number 1 must be done first. The person, or department, who does the activity, appears in the top right section of the box, as in Figure 2.6.

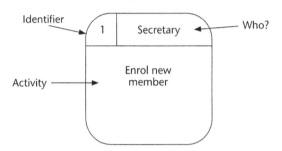

Figure 2.6
Process box.

Data flows

Data flows show the movement of data around the system. They take the form of an arrow which shows the direction of the data. Data flows should be labelled to show exactly what data is flowing. For example, 'medical card' might be the label attached to a data flow in the Medical Centre.

External entities

These are people or organizations outside of the system being investigated. They will send data into the system or receive data from it. At Swillbuckets, 'artiste' would be an external entity, as would 'brewery'. They are shown in the form of ovals with a label inside. If the same entity appears more than once on a diagram, it has a line through it. Figure 2.7 shows the entity 'member'.

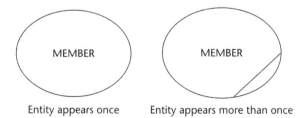

Figure 2.7
External entities.

Data stores

These are places where data is stored. For example, an Orders file would be a data store. Jack Trout's members' shoebox at Swillbuckets is a data store, and so is Betty and George's Appointment Book at the Medical Centre. Data stores are represented by open-ended rectangles with a unique reference and a label. Normally, at this stage, the reference will begin with 'M' for 'Manual'. Figure 2.8 shows how Jack's members' shoebox might look.

Figure 2.8
Data store – Jack's
shoebox.

M1	Members' details

So, now we know the components of a DFD, let's see what they look like when we put them together. Figure 2.9 shows part of a DFD for Swillbuckets and Figure 2.10 shows part of one for the Medical Centre. Note that these are not yet complete DFDs.

Figure 2.9
Partial DFD –
Swillbuckets.

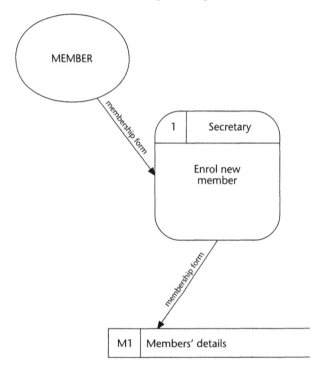

Data flow diagram rules
The analyst needs to be aware of some rules which apply to DFDs. These rules exist not to make life difficult, but to ensure consistency in diagramming.

Process rules
- Processes must have both inputs and outputs. If there is no input, but there is an output, then the output has been created from thin air. Sadly, this does not happen. If there is an input but no output, then the process is a waste of everyone's time and should be scrapped.

Data flow rules
- Data flows must go through a process box. It is not allowed to have a data flow going directly from an external entity to a data store, for example.

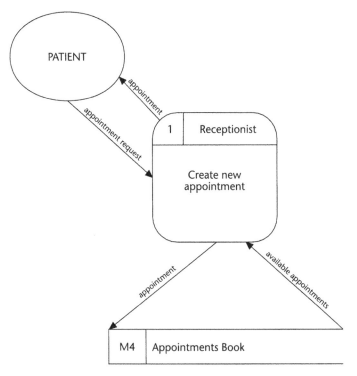

Figure 2.10
Partial DFD – Medical
Centre.

External entity rules
● The label must be a noun, e.g. SUPPLIER.

Data store rules
● A data flow into a data store means update the data store.

● A data flow from a data store means retrieve data from the data store.

Context diagram
This is the first diagram we draw. We only need to draw one of these because it shows the entire system. In order to prevent it looking too complicated, we might summarize the key data flows. All the processes in the system are contained in one process box. The aim is to get an overview of which external entities send or receive data from our system at present. In other words, a context diagram is a tool to establish the scope of the system under investigation. It is similar to a DFD, but does not obey the rules outlined above.

Document flow diagram
This follows on from the context diagram. It looks inside the one process box in the context diagram and breaks it up into departments or areas of work. It also allows us to show exactly which parts of the overall system we are going to investigate. Some parts might not need looking at.

2.3.4 Simple steps in data flow modelling

The main tasks to be completed, in order, are:

1 Draw a context diagram.

2 Draw a document flow diagram.

3 Draw a top-level data flow diagram.

4 Draw lower level data flow diagrams.

These main tasks will be split up into a number of smaller, simple tasks. An example from the Medical Centre will be given at each stage.

1 List of external entities

Make a list of all the things (entities) external to our organization which send data to us or receive data from us. The Medical Centre list might consist of:

- **Patient**: the Centre will receive all kinds of data from patients, such as appointment requests.

- **University**: the Centre receives a list of new students.

- **General Practitioners Council**: the Centre sends to the GPC timesheets for the work done by the receptionists and the Nurse. Doctors are paid according to the number of patients on their list. The Centre receives pay slips from the GPC.

- **Supplier**: Nurse Payne will send orders for supplies and receive invoices.

- **Hospital**: the Centre sends referrals to the hospital and receives reports on treatment at the hospital.

- **Prescription Monitoring Agency**: the Centre sends the PMA data on prescriptions and receives reports on the practice for prescribing drugs nationally.

- **Accountant**: the Centre sends regular financial information and receives reports.

You may wish to draw a table like that in Table 2.1. Remember to draw it from the point of view of the system under investigation.

2 Draw the context diagram

This follows easily from the table: see Figure 2.11.

Notice that a dashed line has been drawn between GPC and the Patient, to show the Medical Card. A dashed line can be used in this way to show data flows between external entities which are felt to be important enough to show.

3 Identify internal areas/departments

Having considered the external data flows, we move on to the internal ones which will appear in the document flow diagram. We need to identify the

Table 2.1 *Data flows and entities.*

External entity	Data flow	Sends (S) or Receives (R)
Patient	Registration form	R
	Appointment request	R
	Appointment	S
	Prescription	S
GPC	Payslips	R
	Patient lists	S
	Timesheets	S
University	Student lists	R
Hospital	Referral	S
	Referral results	R
PMA	Prescriptions	S
	Prescription reports	R
Suppliers	Catalogues	R
	Orders	S
	Invoices	R
Accountant	Financial details	S
	Finance reports	R

internal areas which might send data between themselves. For example, in a college or university the areas might be: Department, Student, Tutor, Admin, Support and so on. In the Medical Centre, the areas might be: Reception, Doctor and Nurse. We need to separate Doctor and Nurse because they perform different tasks for the Centre. We also need to identify the data flows between these areas, as we did with the Context Diagram. You could draw a table as in the previous section, but in this case it's fairly simple, so we'll draw the diagram.

4 Draw the document flow diagram

The document flow diagram need not just consist of documents. Confusingly, it can include any type of data flow – electronic, word of mouth, or, in George's case, arm-waving histrionics which communicate very little. Nurse Payne, on the other hand, can sometimes communicate a huge amount of information with just one look. It differs from a data flow diagram in that it does not include any processes, as shown in Figure 2.12.

The system boundary has been added to show exactly what areas we are concerned with in the Medical Centre. All entities outside of the dashed line are external entities. It should be obvious from the Context Diagram which areas are outside our system. With the user's agreement, it is the analyst's role to investigate the internal entities. In this case, they are RECEPTIONIST, DOCTOR and NURSE.

Figure 2.11
Context diagram for
the Medical Centre.

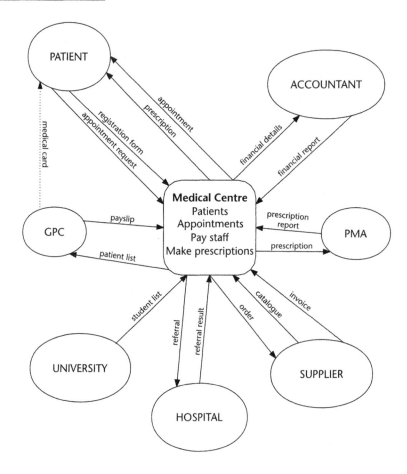

5 **Convert the document flow diagram into a top-level data flow diagram**

● Start with the document flow diagram.

● Focus on the sources/recipients (ellipses) inside the boundary. In our example (Figure 2.12), these are: Doctor, Nurse and Reception. Now look at the data flows coming into and going out of these ellipses.

● What processes generate these data flows? What are the main processes carried out by Doctor, Nurse and Reception?

● Let's take Reception – we might start with the data flow 'appointment'. What process generates this 'appointment'? Remember that we're trying to be general at the moment, so we could identify a process called 'Process Appointment'. This would cover a number of our data flows.

● Another data flow is 'registration form'. What process generates 'registration form'? Being general again, we might call it 'Register Patient'.

● Other data flows are 'prescription' and 'referral'. What processes generate these? They could be brought together under the process 'Process Patient Requirements'.

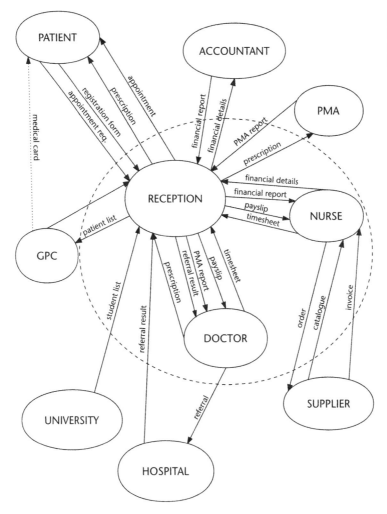

Figure 2.12
Document flow
diagram for the
Medical Centre.

● Many of the other data flows concerning Reception are sending or receiving information to or from external organizations like the GPC. These could all come under the umbrella of a process called 'Process Management Information'. That covers Reception. In fact, the only data flows not covered by these general process headings are the Nurse's dealings with suppliers. We could put these data flows into a process called, say, 'Maintain Supplies'.

● Put these general processes together in one diagram and we have our DFD. For the sake of simplicity, data stores can be left out of this top-level diagram. They will appear in the lower level diagrams.

We now have an overview DFD. This is normally called a Level 1 DFD. Figure 2.13 shows the complete Level 1 DFD.

Notice that the GPC entity has a line through it to indicate that it appears at least twice in the diagram. The label 'Current Physical DFD' indicates that the diagram shows the current state of affairs and that we are looking at the

Figure 2.13
Level 1 current
physical DFD for the
Medical Centre.

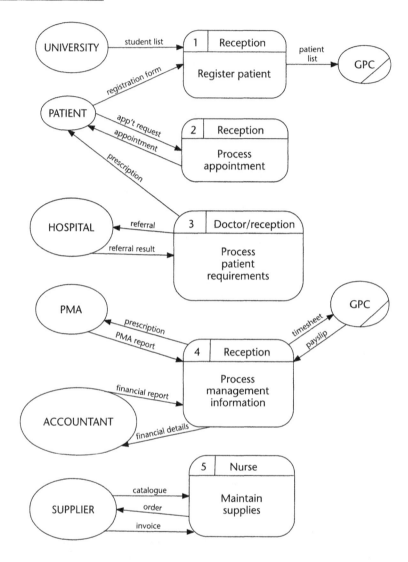

physical view of how things happen. Who does what? When? How? Later on, we'll 'logicalize' these diagrams and focus on *what* is actually achieved.

6 Develop the lower level DFDs using functional decomposition

What is functional decomposition? The Level 1 DFD gives us a very general overview of what goes on in the Medical Centre, but provides no details about what really happens. We need to know these details. So we need to talk to the users again to gain a deeper understanding of what happens at a lower level.

This enables us to create lower level diagrams, working down from the Level 1 processes. Thus each Level 1 process might be broken down into a number of Level 2 processes. The example in Figure 2.14 shows the Level 1 process 'Process appointments' and how it might look when broken down into more detailed processes at Level 2.

Functional decomposition

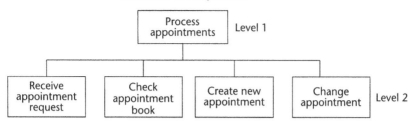

Figure 2.14
Decomposition of
DFDs – Levels 1 and
2.

These Level 2 processes must now be incorporated into a full DFD for each Level 1 process. So, in our example, we will need five Level 2 DFDs, because there are five Level 1 processes to decompose.

This decomposition process can continue to even lower levels. It may be the case that some processes are still not fully broken down even at Level 2. For example, in Figure 2.14 there is a Level 2 process called 'Receive appointment request'. This is a little vague. We could make this process clearer by breaking it up as shown in Figure 2.15.

Functional decomposition

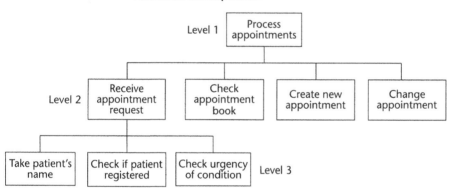

Figure 2.15
Decomposition of
DFDs – Levels 1, 2
and 3.

And so on. We may even want to break down one or two of these processes to make them absolutely clear. It is unlikely, even in the most complex systems, that we would ever go below Level 4. The lowest level processes are known as elementary processes.

When drawing the lower level DFDs, we must now incorporate the data stores. These were omitted from the Level 1 DFD, simply to avoid overloading the diagram. We must also ensure that every data flow and entity on the Level 1 diagram appears somewhere on the lower level ones.

So, let's draw the Level 2 DFDs for the Medical Centre at the University of Life. The first one we'll do is for the Level 1 process 'Register Patient'. This will contain in it four sub-processes numbered 1.1 through to 1.4 (Figure 2.16).

Notice that in Figure 2.16 a numbering system is used. This is necessary so that each process has a unique identifier. The system is easy to follow: the Level 1 number comes first, then the Level 2 number and so on.

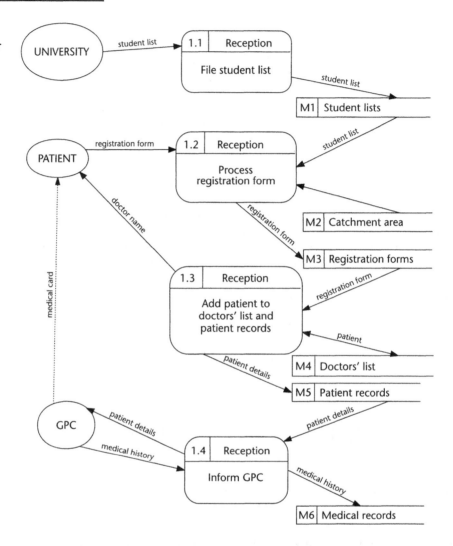

Figure 2.16
Level 2 DFD 'Register Patient'.

A couple of things may need explaining in Figure 2.16. Process 1.1 – 'File student list' – has a data flow from the University. The data flow is the list of new students who have enrolled that year. All Process 1.1 does is to take the list and file it. Even Betty and George can manage that. The list is filed in a data store. In this case it is 'M1 – Student Lists'. 'M' stands for 'manual'. It's a manual store, not an electronic one. It's the first data store we've identified, so that's why it's 'M1'.

Data stores can take many forms. Normally, they will be files or ledgers, that kind of thing. But they could also be forms, catalogues, noticeboards, or anywhere data is held.

This DFD is very simple; none of the processes have more than two or three inputs and outputs, so there is no need to break it down further. These four processes can now be described as elementary processes, i.e. they don't need simplifying.

Let's have a look at the next DFD (Figure 2.17). This one focuses on the appointments process.

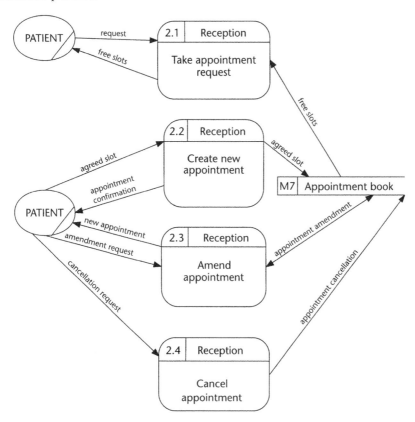

Figure 2.17
Level 2 DFD -
'Process
Appointment'.

Once again, this one is very simple. It's worth bearing in mind that these DFDs are the first attempt at this process. When we show them to users and ask if they are accurate, the users will almost certainly identify some errors in the DFDs, which will need putting right. Also, there are various checks to be done on the DFDs which may well throw up some more problems. So don't think of this process of drawing DFDs as a once only job. It's probably the first of several attempts to get them right.

Next we have process number 3 – 'Process Patient Requirements'. This one illustrates what happens when patients arrive at the Medical Centre for treatment (see Figure 2.18).

This DFD throws up a couple of points. Firstly, notice that the 'appointment' data flow has an arrowhead at both ends. This means that data is taken from the data store 'M7 Appointment book' and also added to it.

Secondly, in creating this DFD, it became apparent that the patient would need to notify the Medical Centre of his or her arrival. This piece of information is missing from the level 1 DFD. We should now go back to the level 1 DFD and add it in. Any data flows to or from external entities must appear in the level 1 DFD and the lower level DFDs. If this doesn't happen, the DFDs will be inconsistent and confusing.

Figure 2.18
Level 2 DFD –
'Process Patient
Requirements'.

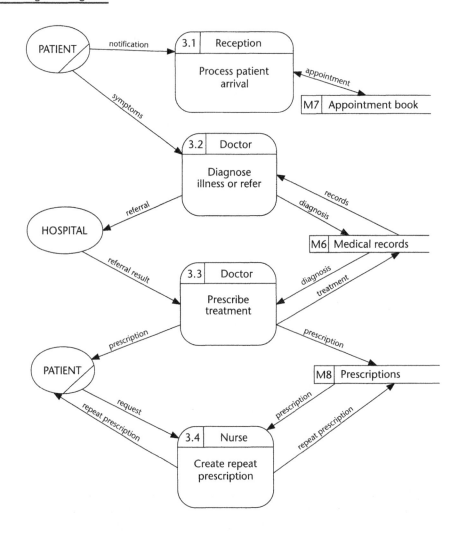

Sometimes the level 2 DFD contains a process which is quite complex and may have several data flows into it and out of it. The next DFD (Figure 2.19) contains such a process.

Process 4.3 – 'Process staff income/expenses' – has three data flows into it and two coming from it. This is a little complex, though some analysts would be happy to leave it alone. However, we will draw a Level 3 DFD to clarify the process.

There is another issue with this DFD. We have a data flow called 'form' coming from 'M11 Expenses forms'. However, nowhere in our DFDs is there a data flow into this data store. So we are taking something from it without ever putting anything into it. Sadly, that kind of thing can't happen. We may therefore need to invent a new process called something like 'Update staff expenses', where we add the expenses forms to the data store. Or we could amend Process 4.2 so that it becomes 'Update staff timesheets and expenses'.

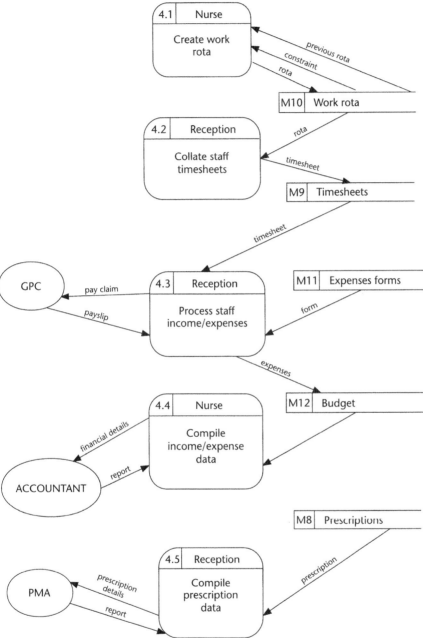

Figure 2.19
Level 2 DFD –
'Process Management
Information'.

Anyway, Figure 2.20 shows how Process 4.3 might look when decomposed to Level 3.

Once again the creation of the DFD reveals something missing. This time it's a data store to store copies of the pay claims sent to the GPC. This would be necessary in case of queries about the pay claims. For example, the GPC might wonder why they are paying the doctors so handsomely when all they do is dispense paracetamol.

Figure 2.20
Level 3 DFD.

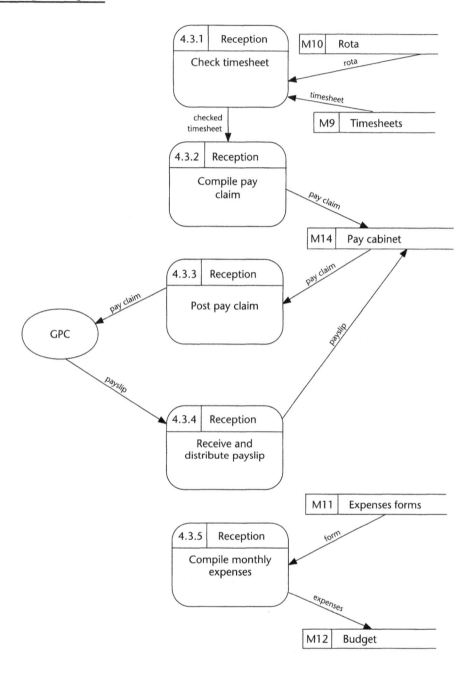

The final Level 2 DFD (Figure 2.21) focuses on Nurse Payne's role as controller of supplies for the Medical Centre.

Our current physical DFDs are now complete. They should give us a picture of what the Medical Centre currently does. They should be understandable and be useful as a communications tool with the user. However, there are limitations with DFDs. They don't do everything (which is why we need other techniques). Here are a few limitations:

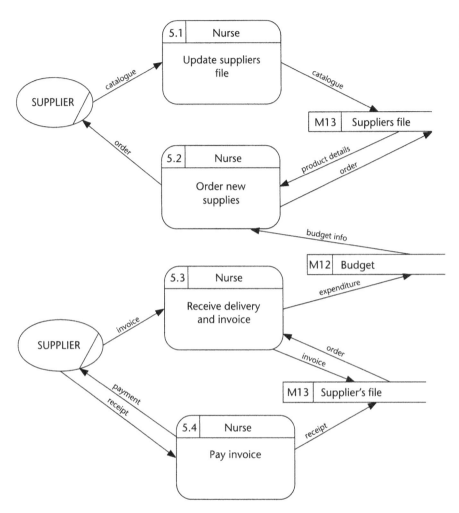

Figure 2.21
Level 2 DFD.

- They don't show us how the data is structured.

- They don't show the effect of time or sequence.

- They may not help communicate with the user – they may be too complex.

- They take a long time to draw and redraw.

- They may never be complete

While these limitations are real enough, the experienced analyst can use DFDs as a useful tool and not allow the limitations to become a problem.

The set of DFDs for the Swillbuckets Case Study are shown in Figures 2.22–2.29.

Figure 2.22
DFDs for the
Swillbuckets case
study (1).

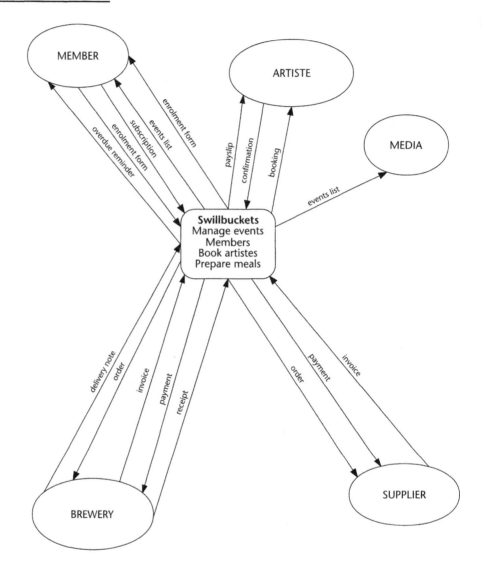

Summary

In this chapter, we have considered the techniques required to analyse a system. Communications skills and data flow modelling have been the focus. The two case studies have been introduced. In the next chapter we look at modelling the data structure.

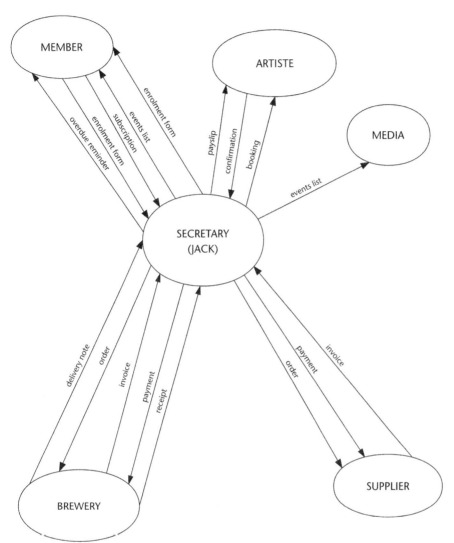

Figure 2.23
DFDs for the
Swillbuckets case
study (2).

Figure 2.24
DFDs for the
Swillbuckets case
study (3).

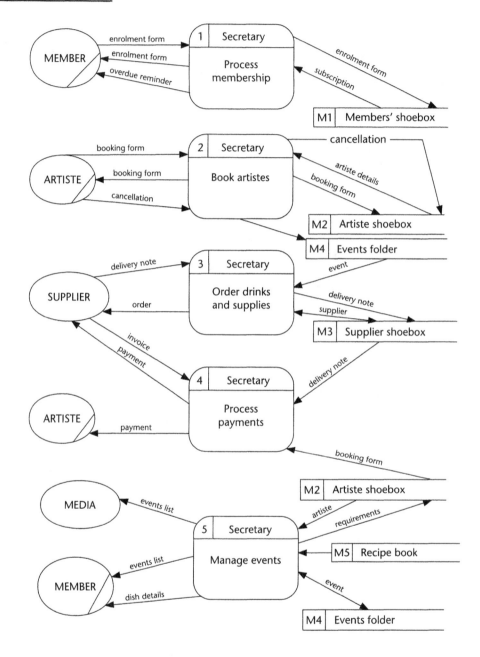

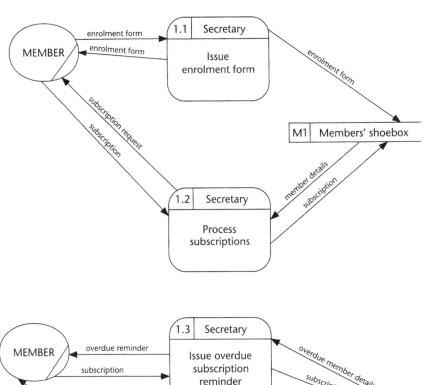

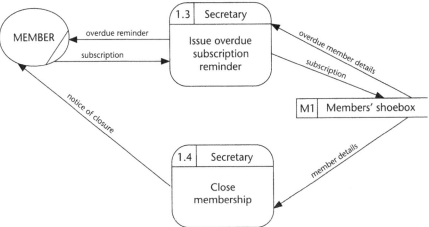

Figure 2.25
DFDs for the
Swillbuckets case
study (4).

Figure 2.26
DFDs for the
Swillbuckets case
study (5).

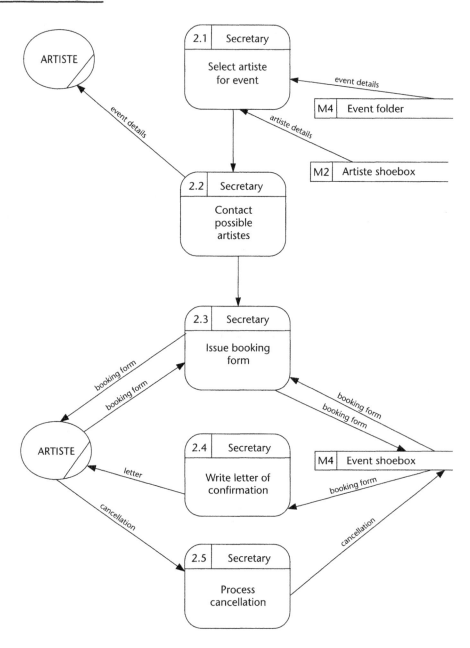

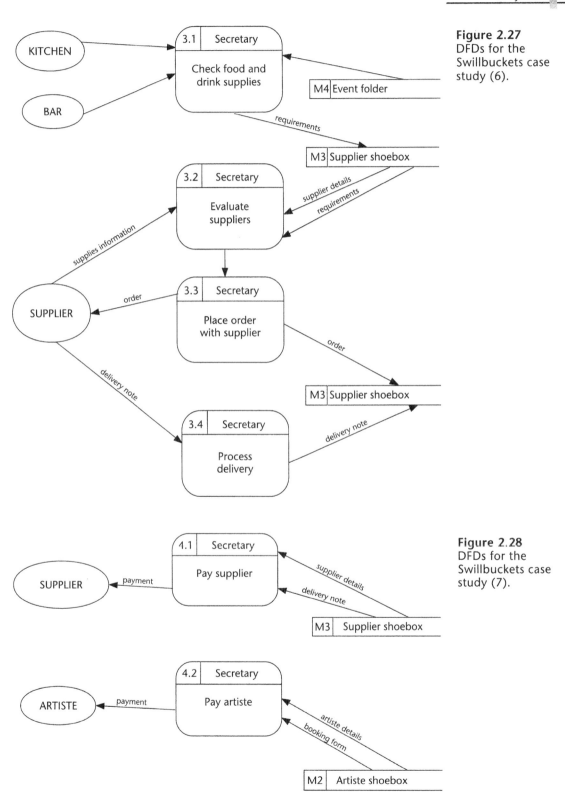

Figure 2.27
DFDs for the Swillbuckets case study (6).

Figure 2.28
DFDs for the Swillbuckets case study (7).

Figure 2.29
DFDs for the
Swillbuckets case
study (8).

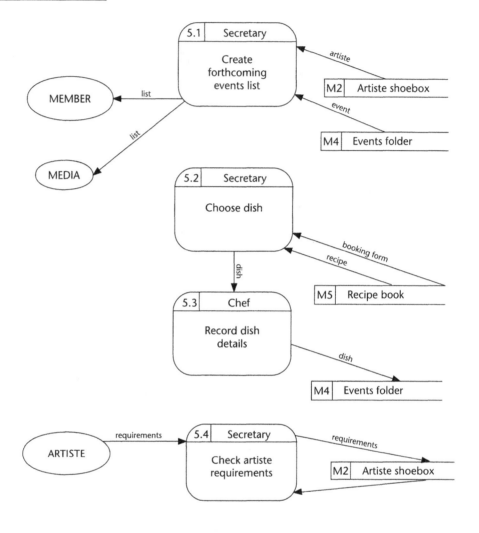

Exercises

2.1 Draw DFDs for each of these scenarios:

(a) A customer goes into a bookshop and asks for this book. The member of staff looks for the book in the online stock catalogue and reports that the book is sold out.

(b) Every month, the Medical Centre receives a list of current drugs available from the drug companies. These lists are collated into a catalogue of drugs which is copied and given to each doctor.

(c) Swillbuckets orders a crate of Babycham from the brewery. Jack Trout fills in an order form and sends copies to the brewery and the barman. The original is kept in the Orders shoebox. When the order arrives, the delivery note is checked against the order form by the barman. If the delivery matches the order, the barman signs the delivery note and attaches it to the order. He sends this to Jack.

(d) Decompose the diagram for part (c) into two lower level DFDs, one showing the order process and one showing the delivery process. Compare them with the top-level DFD in (c).

2.2 Draw a physical DFD to model this vet practice scenario.

Hallam Vets consists of two vets plus a receptionist. Both vets maintain records of treatment sessions. In addition, they maintain detailed animal records held in reception. When an owner arrives with an animal, the receptionist enters new animal details if the animal has not been seen before. The receptionist also reminds owners if their account needs paying, and receives payments where offered. She records details of payments.

Patients may send payments by cheque in the mail, or pay by cheque or cash at reception. Payments are banked daily. Once a week the receptionist checks the payments. She updates the ledgers and records the updated balance on the owner's records. She sends reminders to owners with outstanding balances. Once a year, a breakdown of treatment has to be prepared by each vet and despatched to the Department of Animal Welfare.

CHAPTER 3

Modelling the data structure

3.1 | Entity modelling

Entity modelling is another technique used in Stage 1 of SSADM. As just mentioned in Chapter 2, DFDs show the processes, or functions, involved in a system. They don't tell us much about the structure of the data: what categories of data, for example, there might be in the system. For this aspect of the system, we need to produce an entity model (or Logical Data Model). This model shows the actual data used by an organization and how it links together. Before we look in more detail at entity modelling, let's be clear what we mean by certain terms.

3.1.1 Entities

Entities are things we might want to keep information about. They are usually types of people like CUSTOMER, or objects like PRODUCT. Jack Trout can't move for all the entities at Swillbuckets Club. They're everywhere. He needs to keep information about MEMBERS, RECIPES, EVENTS, ARTISTES and so on. These are all entities. There are four tests we could use to decide whether or not something is an entity:

1 An entity must be important to the organization.

2 An entity must have at least one attribute (see below).

3 An entity must occur more than once – so if MEMBER is to be classed as an entity, there must be more than one member of Swillbuckets. Fortunately, there is more than one, though this could change when the Health Inspectors visit next month.

4 Each entity occurrence must be uniquely identifiable – so we must be able to uniquely identify each member if MEMBER is an entity. This can be done through a Membership Number, for example. Similarly, we could identify a RECIPE through its unique Recipe Name or Recipe Number if there are many of them.

Entities are represented by rectangles with rounded corners in Entity Models, as shown in Figure 3.1. The name of the entity is always singular.

Figure 3.1
The MEMBER entity.

3.1.2 Attributes

Each entity has a number of attributes. These are bits of data associated with the entity. If we take the entity MEMBER at Swillbuckets, we might identify Member Name as an attribute of MEMBER. Other attributes might be:

● Membership Number

● Member Address

● Date of Birth

● Type

● Seconder

● Renewal Date

So the full record for a member, when we add in all the data, might look like that in Table 3.1.

3.1.3 Keys

A key is a way of identifying something – an entity or form or whatever. Your key is your name, usually. It's how other people identify you. But it's not a brilliant key, because there will be lots of people with the same name as you (unless you're called Amanda Stotc). A better key to identify you would be your National Insurance Number (if you live in the UK). It's unique. There are never two the same. That's why you have it. Similar keys can be identified for people living in other countries.

Table 3.1 *A full membership record.*

Attribute	Data
Member Name	Malcolm Sprotdale
Membership Number	3421
Member Address	1 Cemetery Road, Wigginton
Date of Birth	5 October 1912
Type	Free
Seconder	Herbert Woodcock
Renewal Date	6 May 2003

Alternatively, your key could be your name combined with your address as a way of identifying who you are. After all, there are not likely to be two Will Winterbottoms living at Hag End Farm, though it's not impossible. The problem is that people move house, whereas a National Insurance Number always stays the same.

We've just seen that an entity is made up of a number of attributes. To identify that entity, we need a key. Let's think of the entity MEMBER. It may be that Member Name could be the key, but, as we've seen, names on their own are not enough. So we could combine it with Member Address and that would do the trick. This would be a composite key, which means that there is more than one attribute involved in the key.

However, a better key would be Membership Number. This uniquely identifies all the MEMBERs. Indeed, that is it's only purpose. This then would be the **primary key**. It's a simple key, which means it's made up of just one attribute.

3.1.4 Relationships

Entities do not exist in isolation in most systems. They have relationships with other entities. If we think about Swillbuckets, we can see that MEMBER, EVENT and ARTISTE are all linked together. For example,

- Artistes entertain Members

- Members attend Events

- Artistes perform at Events

Similarly,

- Students attend Classes

- Students have Tutors

- Tutors give Classes

- Doctors treat Patients

- Patients make Appointments

- Doctors attend Appointments

The entities are all related in these examples. They are joined together by a verb which describes the relationship between them.

In an entity model, related entities are joined by a line, as in Figure 3.2.

Figure 3.2
Related entities.

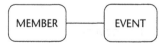

Relationship type
Unfortunately, there are three different types of relationship. These are:

- one-to-one (1:1)

- one-to-many (1:*M*)

- many-to-many (*M:N*)

A one-to-one relationship is fairly unusual. An example might be CAR and DRIVER. This would be one-to-one if a car only had **one** driver and the driver only drove **one** car. But if a car could have more than one driver, it would be one-to-many; and if the same driver could also drive more than one car, it would be many-to-many. Notice in Figure 3.3 how the entity model changes, depending upon the type of relationship.

1:1

A car can have only one driver; a driver can have only one car

1:*M*

A car can have more than one driver; a driver can have only one car

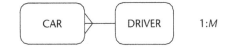

1:*M*

A car can have only one driver; a driver can have more than one car

M:N

A car can have more than one driver; a driver can have more than one car

Figure 3.3
Relationship types.

One-to-many relationships are very common:

- A PATIENT can only have **one** DOCTOR, but a DOCTOR can treat **many** PATIENTs.

- At Swillbuckets, an EVENT presents only **one** ARTISTE, but an ARTISTE can appear at **many** EVENTs.

This could change, of course. Jack Trout might decide to put on more than one ARTISTE at some EVENTs. Then the relationship would become many-to-many. So it is the policies of the organization which determine the type of relationship. (Remember: more than one = many.)

Many-to-many relationships are also quite common:

- A MEMBER might attend **many** EVENTs and each EVENT could have **many** MEMBERs.

- A STUDENT might take **many** COURSES and each COURSE might have **many** STUDENTS.

- A CUSTOMER might buy **many** PRODUCTs and a PRODUCT might be bought by **many** CUSTOMERs.

Sadly, many-to-many relationships are not good for databases. They cannot be implemented effectively. So many-to-many relationships have to be resolved.

3.1.5 Resolving many-to-many relationships

In effect, this means we have to split many-to-many relationships into two one-to-many relationships. This requires us to find a link entity which is a single occurrence of the many-to-many relationship.

1 Find a link entity

Here's an example: let's look at the CUSTOMER:PRODUCT relationship. We've already said it's a many-to-many relationship, so let's think of a link entity. A single occurrence of this relationship might be a TRANSACTION. That is one CUSTOMER buying one PRODUCT. In diagrammatic form, we see how this might work. Each occurrence of TRANSACTION represents one occurrence of the CUSTOMER:PRODUCT relationship. The many-to-many relationship changes to two one-to-many relationships in Figure 3.4.

Figure 3.4
Resolution of many-to-many relationships.

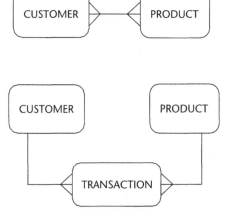

Each CUSTOMER can make **many** transactions, but each TRANSACTION is made by only **one** CUSTOMER. Similarly, Each PRODUCT can be part of **many** transactions, but each TRANSACTION only involves **one** PRODUCT.

Here's another example from an analysis of the Probation Service. Preliminary investigation reveals the entities: COURT and DEFENDANT. But the relationship is many-to-many. Each COURT may have **many** DEFENDANTs and each DEFENDANT can come before **many** COURTs. To resolve this relationship, we need to think of a single instance of the relationship. What is the term for the coming together of COURT and DEFENDANT at a particular moment in time? The answer is TRIAL. TRIAL is the link entity which resolves the many-to-many relationship. For simplicity's sake, we will assume there is only one defendant at a trial, as modelled in Figure 3.5.

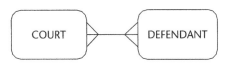

Figure 3.5
The COURT and DEFENDANT relationship.

A single instance of the COURT and DEFENDANT relationship is a TRIAL

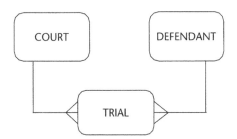

2 Consider the attributes

When we create a new link entity in this way, we need to consider which attributes will make up the new entity. There will be one or two from the original two entities, but there may be some completely new ones. The COURT and DEFENDANT entities might have had these attributes (Keys are underlined):

COURT	**DEFENDANT**
<u>Court Number</u>	<u>Defendant Number</u>
Court Name	Defendant Name
Court Address	Defendant Address
Postcode	Postcode
Court Type	Date of Birth
Court Clerk	Current status

But when we introduce the new link entity, TRIAL, it will normally be the case that the keys from the two original entities will need to be in the TRIAL entity. In order to identify a TRIAL, we need to know the Court Number and the Defendant Number.

So TRIAL might look something like this:

TRIAL
Court Number *
Defendant Number *
<u>Trial Number</u>
Trial Date
Judge
Charge
Defence Lawyer
Prosecutor
Secretary

In this example, Trial Number would be the key. The two keys taken from the COURT and DEFENDANT entities are called **foreign keys** and are usually marked with an asterisk. They could have been used as a key for TRIAL, along with Trial Date, but Trial Number is simpler.

Foreign keys, then, are primary keys in other related entities and are used as a means of linking the entities together.

3.2 | Simple steps in entity modelling

Now that the terms are reasonably clear, let's summarize the steps involved in entity modelling.

1 List the possible entities.
As we've seen, this will be done by talking to the users. It is also necessary to check the DFDs, as we must ensure that we hold information about the external entities identified there, such as ARTISTE.

2 Check that the entities listed are really entities.
This can be done by applying the four rules outlined earlier.

3 Draw a basic entity model, with boxes around the entities.

4 Identify which entities are related.
Draw a line between them.

5 Give the relationship a name in each direction.
This can be quite difficult, as the analyst is attempting to summarize what may be a complex relationship in a short phrase or word. Try to avoid vague names if possible and specify what exactly the relationship is. Figure 3.6 gives a couple of examples.

6 Identify the relationship type.

    (1:1, 1:M or M:N)

7 Resolve any one-to-one relationships.

8 Resolve any many-to-many relationships.
Add in link entities.

9 Add the attributes, including primary keys and foreign keys.

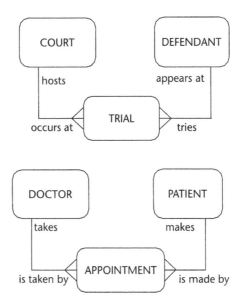

Figure 3.6
Naming the relationships.

The systems analyst will need to communicate regularly with the user during this process in order to check that all necessary entities have been identified and that the relationships are accurate.

3.3 █ Entity modelling at Swillbuckets

Let's go through the simple steps using the Swillbuckets case study. Just as a reminder, Swillbuckets puts on events on a weekly basis for the entertainment of members. These events feature artistes of various types and all manner of barely legal activities – the annual six-legged pig race being a case in point. In addition, Swillbuckets offers certain dishes based on local recipes and a range of local beers and sundry items. One can hardly stress enough the importance of Cooper's 'Old Firtle Ale' to the local economy and social mix.

1   List the possible entities.
One method is to pick out the nouns in the interview transcripts. We are looking for anything which might be important to Jack and other users at Swillbuckets – things they might need to hold information about.
    A quick run through might identify the following candidate entities:

- ARTISTE

- EVENT

- MEMBER

- DISH

- BREWERY

- DRINK

- RECIPE

A glance at the DFDs drawn in the previous chapter reveals that the external entity SUPPLIER needs adding to our list – the suppliers of foodstuffs. Similarly, MEDIA needs considering – information about the local media.

2   Check that the entities are really entities.
The next step is to check that each of these is a real entity. All the candidate entities are important to Swillbuckets, so they all pass test one. Similarly, they all have attributes, so they pass test two. However, test three throws up a problem – do they occur more than once? Since Jack gets all his beers from the same brewery – Cooper's – BREWERY will only occur once. It may be that we can dispense with this one. This is particularly sensible given that we have identified SUPPLIER as an entity. The brewery could be recorded as a supplier. So BREWERY fails the test. They all pass the last test – can they be uniquely identified?

3   Draw the basic entity model.
Now we can draw an entity model showing the eight entities identified so far (Figure 3.7). Bear in mind that there may be more entities to come when we show the user our entity model.

Figure 3.7
Swillbuckets entity
model – boxes.

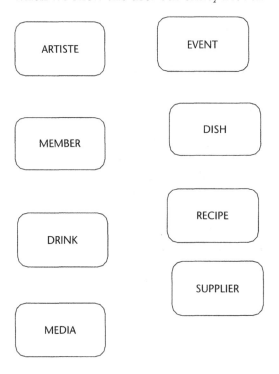

At the moment, all we've done is put boxes around the entities.

4   Identify the relationships.
We'll start with ARTISTE. ARTISTEs attend EVENTs, so there is a relationship between ARTISTE and EVENT. Similarly:

- MEMBERs attend EVENTs

- EVENTs provide DISHes

- DISHes require RECIPEs

- SUPPLIERs supply DRINKs

- MEDIA cover EVENTs

So let's add these relationships into our model (Figure 3.8).

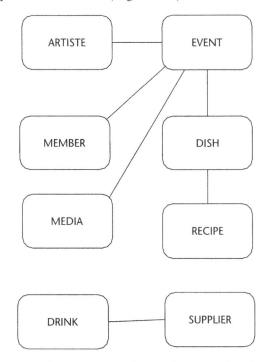

Figure 3.8
Entity model with relationships.

There is a problem here. The DRINK and SUPPLIER relationship is isolated from the other entities. This may be all right, but as analysts we would need to check with Jack and ensure the accuracy of our model. So let's do that.

Jack informs us that we've made a mistake. He further informs us that he's giving us a watch and paying us to tell the time – whatever that means. Basically we've missed out the information about the supplies he gets from the SUPPLIER, the stuff that goes into the dishes. Also, why does he need to keep information about drinks? He already knows everything about drinks. It transpires that really what Jack needs is information about ORDERs – whether it's ORDERs for drinks or from food suppliers. Even if Tommy Chillmore turns up at the back door with a bag of wet fish, that could still be recorded as an ORDER – the amount, the cost etc. So let's have another crack at the entity model (Figure 3.9).

Notice that ORDER is linked to RECIPE at the moment because RECIPEs require ORDERs. However, the orders for drinks have nothing to do with the RECIPEs, so there's another problem. It looks like we need a separate

Figure 3.9
Revised entity model
with relationships.

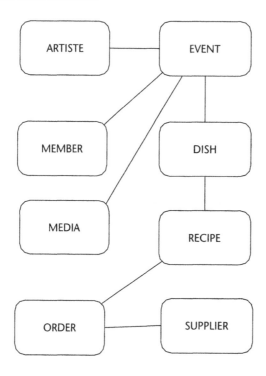

entity for drink orders. The key thing here is not to worry about the odd mistake. As long as we are beginning to understand the data and how it is related, the problems should be overcome. Let's create an entity called DRINK ORDERS and put that in our model (Figure 3.10).

That looks fine for now.

5   Give the relationships a name.
This needs to be done in each direction. For example, suppliers SUPPLY food and food IS SUPPLIED BY suppliers. Let's amend the entity model (Figure 3.11).

6   Identify the type of relationship.
In this step, we need to look at each relationship in turn and decide whether it is 1:1, 1:*M* or *M:N*.

● ARTISTE and EVENT: the current situation is that each ARTISTE might perform at **many** EVENTS, but each EVENT will only present **one** ARTISTE. So the relationship is 1:*M*. However, we should bear in mind that in the future Jack might want to have more than one ARTISTE per event. This may end up being a requirement for the design of the new system.

● EVENT and MEMBER: each MEMBER might attend **many** EVENTs and each EVENT will attract **many** MEMBERs. This is therefore an *M:N* type of relationship. We will need to look at this relationship again shortly.

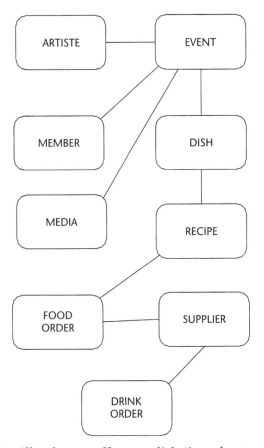

Figure 3.10
Revised entity model.

- EVENT and DISH: each EVENT will only ever offer **one** dish (in order to keep Freddo Smitho just the right side of sane) and each dish will be offered at **many** EVENTs. So it's a 1:*M* relationship.

- DISH and RECIPE: each DISH is produced from **one** RECIPE and each RECIPE prescribes **one** DISH. This is a 1:1 relationship. In this circumstance, it is usually possible to combine the entities into one. In this case we could keep the entity DISH, but make Recipe Number an attribute of DISH. We would need to check if this attribute is needed with Jack or Freddo.

- EVENT and MEDIA: each MEDIA branch (or MEDIUM) will cover **many** EVENTs and each EVENT may be covered by **many** MEDIA branches. This is an *M:N* relationship in its current form and will need further consideration.

- RECIPE and FOOD ORDER: each RECIPE could require **many** FOOD ORDERs and each FOOD ORDER could be required for **many** RECIPES. This is clearly a many-to-many relationship and will also need looking at again.

- SUPPLIER and FOOD ORDER: each SUPPLER might deal with **many** FOOD ORDERS but each FOOD ORDER will only be placed with **one** SUPPLIER. It's a one-to-many relationship.

Figure 3.11
Entity model with
relationship names.

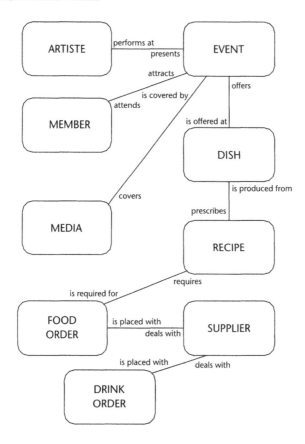

- SUPPLIER and DRINK ORDER: same as for SUPPLIER and FOOD ORDER.

Let's see how this step affects our entity model (Figure 3.12).

7 Resolve any one-to-one relationships.
We do have one such relationship, between DISH and RECIPE. We will need to discuss this with Jack and Freddo. Freddo informs us, to no one's great surprise, that he doesn't bother much with recipes. He makes it up as he goes along. So there's very little point in storing information about recipes.

However, Jack would like to know how much meat is in stock, so that he doesn't order more than he needs. Only the other week, Jack had ordered 50 kg of beef in preparation for Freddo's 'Industrial strength chilli'. Imagine his surprise when he discovered that there was already 35 kg in the freezer!

What Jack needs is information about the ingredients and how much there is in stock. It seems that we have lost one entity (RECIPE), but found another (INGREDIENT). Let's make these changes in the entity model (Figure 3.13).

The relationship between INGREDIENT and DISH turns out to be many-to-many. This is because each DISH contains **many** INGREDIENTs and each INGREDIENT is contained in **many** DISHes. For example, the INGREDIENT 'beef flavouring' appears in most of Freddo's dishes, including even 'Omelette Carbonari'.

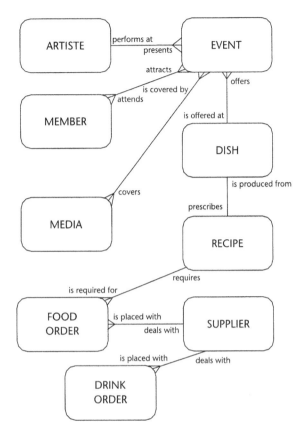

Figure 3.12
Entity model with
type of relationship.

Similarly, INGREDIENT and FOOD ORDER is many-to-many, since each INGREDIENT can appear on **many** FOOD ORDERS and each FOOD ORDER can be have **many** INGREDIENTS on it. Clearly, we have some work to do in the next step.

8 Resolve any many-to-many relationships.
We have a few of these, so let's take them one at a time: firstly, the EVENT–MEMBER relationship. In order to resolve many-to-many relationships, we need to find a link entity. It's often useful to try to think of a single instance of the relationship. In this case, it will be something along the lines of a member's attendance at an event. If, for example, Jack were to issue a ticket for an event, the information on the ticket would be just the sort of information we're looking for. So we might call the link entity EVENT TICKET. The information associated with this entity (its attributes) might be: the title of the event, the date of the event, the member number and the ticket number. So we have some information about the EVENT, some information about the MEMBER and a unique identifier (ticket number).

However, *Jack does not currently do this*. We must check with Jack that he is happy collecting and storing this information. It should be noted in the Problem/Requirement List and considered in Stage 2 (Chapter 4). We must

Figure 3.13
Entity model with
one-to-one
relationships
resolved.

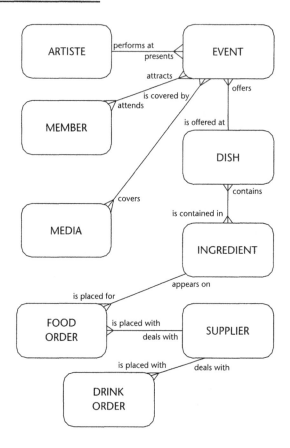

bear in mind that we are modelling the current system at this stage. In resolving many-to-many relationships, we may be making assumptions about the new system. We must be careful not to do this without verifying these assumptions. These assumptions will have to be examined again when we consider the Problem/Requirement List. If necessary, we can leave a many-to-many relationship unresolved for the time being and return to it in the Design Stage.

The next relationship is EVENT and MEDIA. We could resolve this by introducing a link entity called, perhaps, COVERAGE, where we store information about the MEDIA coverage of each EVENT. However, this seems like information overload. Does Jack really store such detailed information about each of his events? When this question was put to Jack he felt that many events were best not covered at all: 'The less people know about last year's six-legged pig race the better'. All Jack does is keep some contact information, so he can phone them to advertise events. It is not a requirement to store any more information. We can, therefore, assume that MEDIA no longer has any links with the main system being analysed.

The next relationship is a little more complex – DISH and INGREDIENT. Let's look carefully at the attributes that these two entities might have (Figure 3.14).

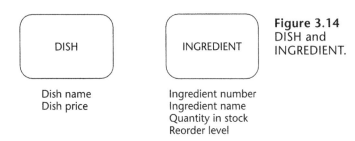

Figure 3.14
DISH and
INGREDIENT.

We have information about the dish and information about the ingredient, but what we don't have is information about which ingredient goes in which dish and how much of it goes in. This is starting to sound a little bit like a recipe, which we've already dismissed, but it's not quite the same. The link entity might be called DISH DETAIL and it will simply be a single instance of the DISH–INGREDIENT relationship. So if the DISH is 'Skewered kidneys in lager', the ingredient might be 'kidneys' and we might store the quantity required for, say, 100 meals, which might be '50 kg'. The next record in DISH DETAIL might be 'Skewered kidneys in lager' again for the DISH, but the INGREDIENT might be 'lager' and the quantity might be '10 litres'. Figure 3.15 shows the link entity and its attributes. Again, this will need noting in the Problem/Requirements List, but we will include the change in our entity model for the time being.

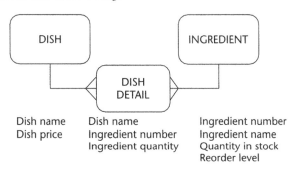

Figure 3.15
DISH and
INGREDIENT
resolved.

Finally, there's FOOD ORDER and INGREDIENT. A single instance of this relationship might be thought of as a FOOD ORDER LINE. If you imagine an order with a list of ingredients on the order, then one line of this list would be our link entity. The information involved might be the Order Number, the Ingredient Number, the Quantity and the Price.

So our latest entity model will look like Figure 3.16.

This is still early days in the modelling process. There will be more changes to come as we start to design the new system.

9 Add the attributes and keys.

It is useful, now that the entity model is nearing completion, to consider the attributes for each entity and which attributes might be the key for each entity. Figure 3.17 gives a rough idea of how this might look.

There are a few things to notice here:

Figure 3.16
Current entity model.

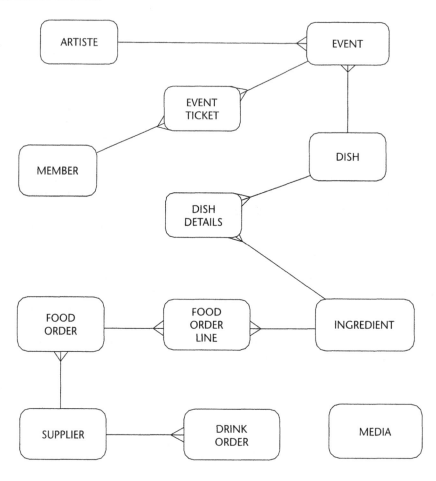

- Primary keys are underlined.

- Attribute names have been condensed into one word with no spaces – spaces can cause problems in some systems. Capital letters are used to denote a new word in the name.

- An asterisk denotes a foreign key – an attribute which acts as a link to another entity by appearing in both. It's a primary key in one entity but not in the other.

- Address attributes are shown as just one attribute, but in reality they are usually made up of a number of attributes e.g. Street, Town, County, Postcode.

We now have an overview of how the data in the current system at Swillbuckets could usefully be structured. In the process we have learnt a lot about the system and how it might be improved. Before we set about making some improvements, there is one final technique which brings together what we have done in chapters 2 and 3 – physical data store/entity cross-reference.

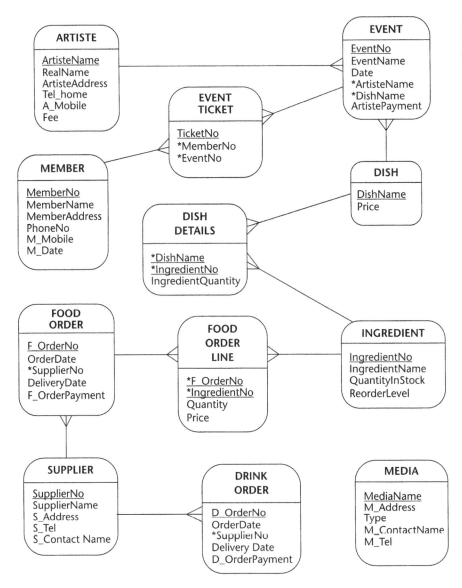

Figure 3.17
Entity model with attributes.

3.4 Physical data store/entity cross-reference

This is an important technique which serves to check that all the data stored in current data stores appears somewhere on our entity model. If it doesn't, we've missed something. Either we have a data store we don't use, or our entity model is not complete. Here are the simple steps in creating the cross-reference:

1 List all the data stores.
This is done by checking the current physical data flow diagrams. For Swillbuckets, the list will look like this:

M1   Membership shoebox
M2   Artiste shoebox
M3   Supplier shoebox
M4   Events folder
M5   Recipe book

2   Cross reference each data store with corresponding entities from the entity model.

This means checking that each data store on the DFDs has a corresponding entity or entities. A data store can have more than one entity. The cross-reference for Swillbuckets appears in Figure 3.18.

Figure 3.18
Data store/entity
cross-reference.

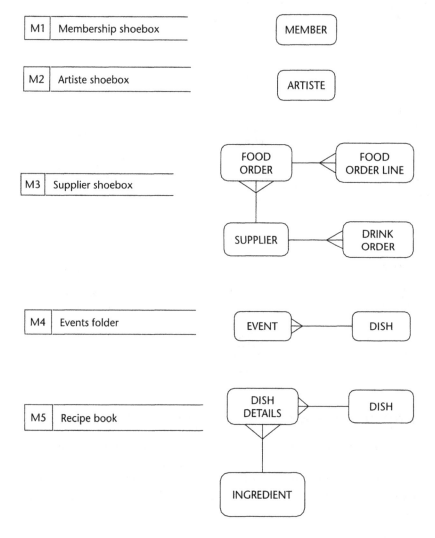

3   Check that each data store has at least one entity.
We can see that this is the case for Swillbuckets.

4   Check that each entity is stored in a data store.

We note that the entities EVENT TICKET and MEDIA do not have data stores. The fact that EVENT TICKET does not have a data store is expected. This is because Jack does not currently store this information and it appears on the entity model to resolve a many-to-many relationship. At some point, we will have to decide, in consultation with Jack, whether to keep it or not.

The fact that the MEDIA entity does not have a data store is the result of an omission on the DFDs. In order to alert the media about his forthcoming events, Jack would have to look up information such as addresses and phone numbers. This information might be stored in an address book or a folder. Either way, it's a data store and should have appeared on the DFDs. We should now add it in, both to the cross-reference and the DFDs. We will call it M6 – Media Details. Our final cross-reference will look like the one in Figure 3.19.

We have now completed our investigation into the current physical system at Swillbuckets. In this chapter we have developed an entity model, so that we know the structure of the data currently in use, and a cross-reference to check that we have done the job properly.

The entity model and cross-reference for the Medical Centre are included in Figures 3.20 and 3.21. Note that M14 'Pay cabinet' has no corresponding entity. This indicates that it does not store any meaningful data and can probably be dispensed with. It will be investigated as part of the next Stage.

In the next chapter we will look at the techniques involved in converting to a logical system and summarizing the requirements for the new system.

Summary

In this chapter, we have looked at the techniques involved in modelling the data. Entity modelling has been the focus and we have considered the elements involved in the structure of data. In the next chapter, we attempt to take a logical view of the data and the data flows.

Figure 3.19
Final data store/entity
cross-reference.

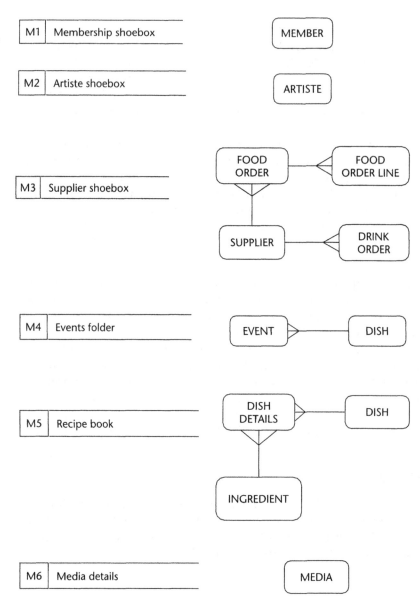

| M1 | Membership shoebox |

MEMBER

| M2 | Artiste shoebox |

ARTISTE

| M3 | Supplier shoebox |

| M4 | Events folder |

| M5 | Recipe book |

| M6 | Media details |

MEDIA

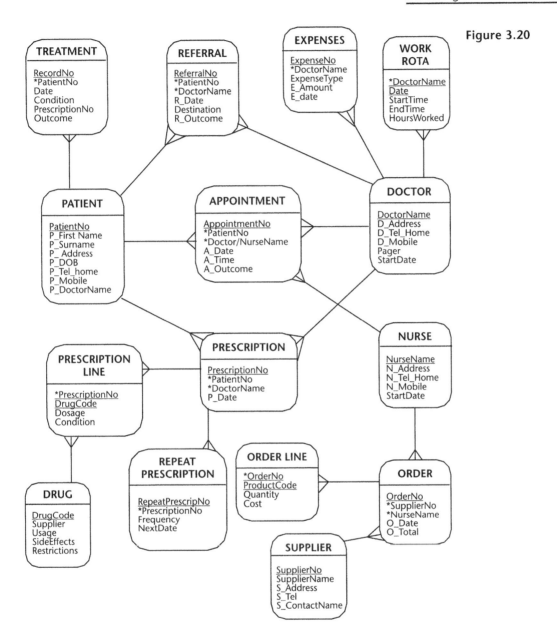

Figure 3.20

Figure 3.21

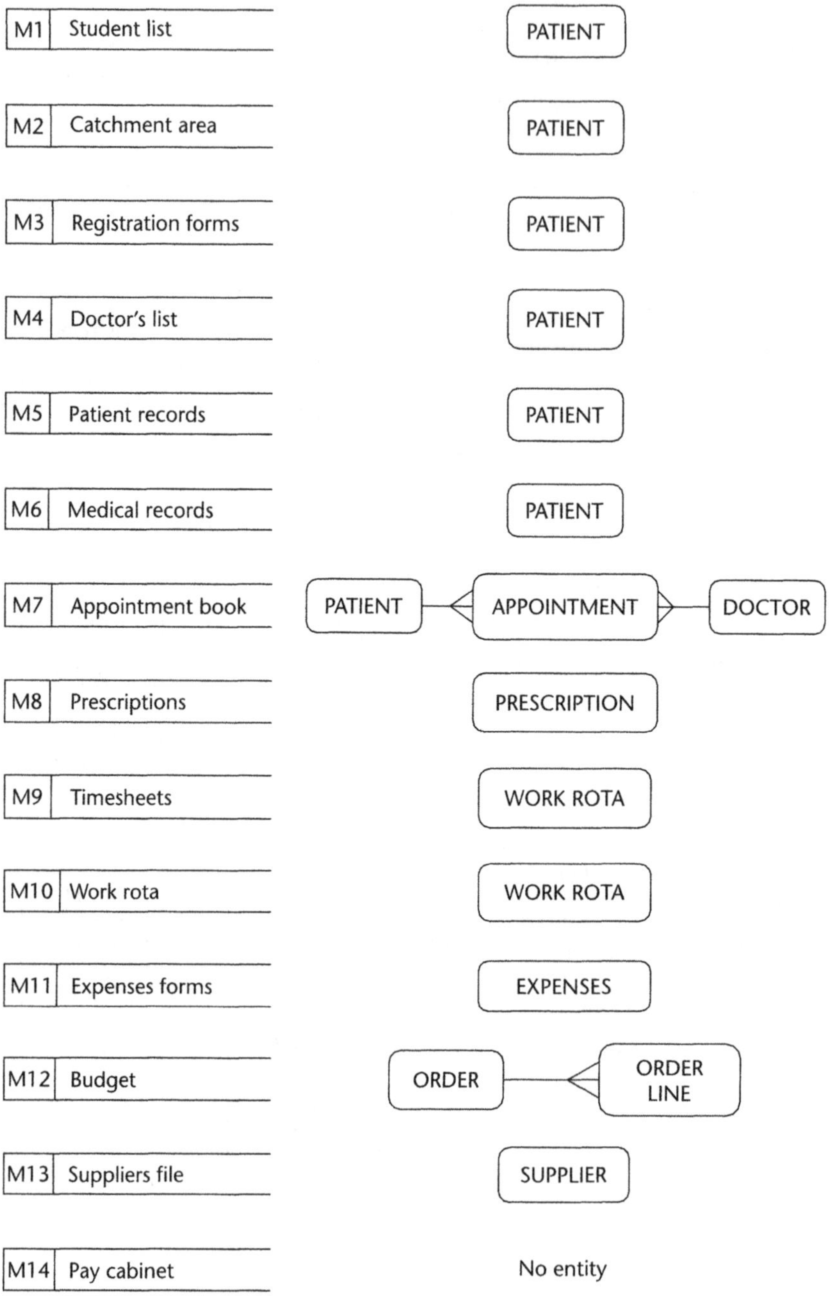

| M1 | Student list |

PATIENT

| M2 | Catchment area |

PATIENT

| M3 | Registration forms |

PATIENT

| M4 | Doctor's list |

PATIENT

| M5 | Patient records |

PATIENT

| M6 | Medical records |

PATIENT

| M7 | Appointment book |

PATIENT ◁— APPOINTMENT —▷ DOCTOR

| M8 | Prescriptions |

PRESCRIPTION

| M9 | Timesheets |

WORK ROTA

| M10 | Work rota |

WORK ROTA

| M11 | Expenses forms |

EXPENSES

| M12 | Budget |

ORDER ◁— ORDER LINE

| M13 | Suppliers file |

SUPPLIER

| M14 | Pay cabinet |

No entity

Exercises

3.1 Draw an entity model to model the following car rental business scenario:

- Cars are always rented from one location and are brought back to the same location.

- Customers may pay by cash or credit card.

- Customers who call the agency may request a particular car make, model etc. if available.

- A bill is presented to the customer prior to releasing the rental car.

- A further bill may be presented to the customer once the rented car has been returned to cover any damage or excessive mileage.

3.2 Draw an entity model to model this university scenario:

- A university department employs lecturers and clerical staff.

- It offers a three-year degree.

- A student has to take 12 modules during the course.

- Each lecturer teaches one or more courses.

- Courses may be taught by more than one lecturer.

- During the year, each postgraduate student has to complete two or three coursework assignments for each module.

CHAPTER 4

The logical view

4.1 | Logicalization

So far, we have been concerned with how the current system works. Before we can design a new and better system, we need to be clear exactly what the current system does, *not* how it does it. In other words, we need to strip off all the physical trappings introduced by Jack Trout at Swillbuckets and the receptionists at the Medical Centre and focus on what the systems actually do. This process is called logicalization, and the outcome will be a logical model of the current system. We try to envisage how things would work if no physical constraints existed. Once it is done, we can move on to Stage 2 of SSADM, where we start to consider how we can improve things.

Logicalization focuses on the data flow diagrams, specifically the lowest level DFDs. The diagrams produced so far use terms and processes created by the users (Jack and the receptionists). These may not be entirely logical. They may be plain daft. Ways of doing things will have developed over the years which might seem fine to the user, but they should at least be examined to see if they are sensible. At the Medical Centre, for example, patient records are made up of handwritten cards stuffed into a cardboard folder. These are then stored in huge filing cabinets, each the size of a small garage. These records will still have to be stored in our new system, but probably not in this way.

The process can be divided up into four steps:

1 **Logicalize the data stores**: as well as the DFDs, logicalization uses the data store/entity cross-reference produced at the end of the last chapter. This cross-reference was physical, so we need to produce a logical version. In this version, each data store will be an entity, or a group of related entities. So we might well end up with a data store called 'Patient' which will contain all the data about patients. So physical stores like 'Student lists', 'Medical Records' and 'Patient Records' will all fall into the logical 'Patient' data store.

As we logicalize the data stores, their labels will change from M1, M2, ... to D1, D2, ... – this indicates that the label no longer signifies a manual data store, just a data store. The exact nature of the data store is not important in a logical DFD.

2   **Remove physical time dependencies**: this involves removing any processes which exist purely as a result of physical time constraints or from convenience. For example, we have a process at the Medical Centre: 4.3.3 – Post pay claim. This process is purely a physical restraint and involves the receptionists waiting until all the timesheets are completed before physically posting the pay claim. In the world of the computer we probably won't be posting much at all. So logically we can remove this process.

3   **Logicalize the processes**: processes in the physical DFDs tell us how physically a process is done and who does the process, but in the logical DFDs this isn't necessary. Logically, processes can be done anyhow by anyone. Logical processes will input data, read it, change it, store it or delete it. Anything to do with physical tasks like Receptionist: 'Receive and distribute payslip' can be removed.

4   **Logicalize the data flows**: any reference to forms, reports, sheets etc. must be removed and replaced with the actual data which flows around the system. The actual data is modelled in the entity model. Thus the data flows will be labelled with the entity used by the process. For example, a patient's medical card will become simply 'patient' or 'patient details' in our logical model. This is imprecise because the medical card will only contain some of the data stored in the PATIENT entity, but to specify which attributes the medical card actually contains would make the diagram too cluttered.

4.2 ▌ Simple steps in logicalization

In this section, the focus will revert to the Medical Centre, though all the documentation for Swillbuckets will be included at the end.

1   Consider the data stores.
We could simply take the entity model (see Figure 3.20) and make each entity a data store. That would be the easiest thing to do and may well be the best thing to do. In the case of the Medical Centre, that would give us 15 logical data stores, which seems reasonable enough. However, it might be worth considering whether to combine some data stores. For example, we might combine all the prescription information into one data store. On the entity model we have 'Prescription', 'Prescription Line' and 'Repeat Prescription' all containing information about prescriptions. We could lump these three together and call them 'Prescription'. We will still need them as separate entities, but joining them together will make the DFDs simpler. This is just a convenient way of representing the data stores; we are not actually merging the entities.

Similarly, 'Doctor' and 'Nurse' are closely related and could be lumped together to form one data store. We would be in big trouble with Nurse Payne if we called this store 'Doctor', so we had better call it 'Doctor/Nurse'. We could also put 'Work Rota' and 'Expenses' in here, as they too refer to the doctors and the nurse.

'Order' and 'Order Line' could sensibly be referred to as the 'Order' data store and finally it might be easier to put 'Referral' and 'Treatment' in with 'Patient' as they all relate to the patient. We might call this store 'Patient'.

2 Produce the logical data store/entity cross-reference.
This is simply a matter of listing the entities and corresponding data stores. Each entity must appear in only one data store. The data stores are labelled 'D1', 'D2' etc. on the logical DFDs.

3 Remove time dependencies.
There are a few of these in our physical DFDs – 4.3.3 'Post pay claim' has already been mentioned, and 4.3.4 'Receive and distribute payslips' is not a process we would want to keep if we could erase it. This is not because we don't want to pay the doctors (though the GPC has considered this approach). It is rather that it serves no logical purpose: it just wastes time by passing on data which could go directly to the doctors. So we can remove some processes in this way.

4 Remove names and departments from the process boxes.
Since it does not matter, logically, who does what, we can take out these labels from the process boxes.

5 Change processes so that they describe what is done to the data.
Where a process refers to any particular ways of doing things instead of what is actually done, we need to change the process to make it logical. An example of this and the previous step is shown in Figure 4.2.

In this example, what we are actually doing is creating a new patient. Whether this is done by adding data to doctors' lists or patient records, or both, should not matter. We are focusing on what happens, not how it is done.

6 Remove any physical references from the process box.
Any process names which refer to physical objects or describe physical actions must be changed. If possible, make the objects entities and make the actions one of: create, update, edit, delete or something similar.

For example, process 4.2 'Collate staff timesheets' might become something like 'Update work rota', since the timesheet information (hours worked per day) is contained in the Work Rota entity in our entity model.

7 Make sure that the data flows refer to logical items of data
These will normally be entities as items of data are contained within entities and not things like forms, reports, handwritten notes, or chewed up pieces of card.

8 Data flows between processes should be removed.
Instead, the data should be directed into and out of a data store.

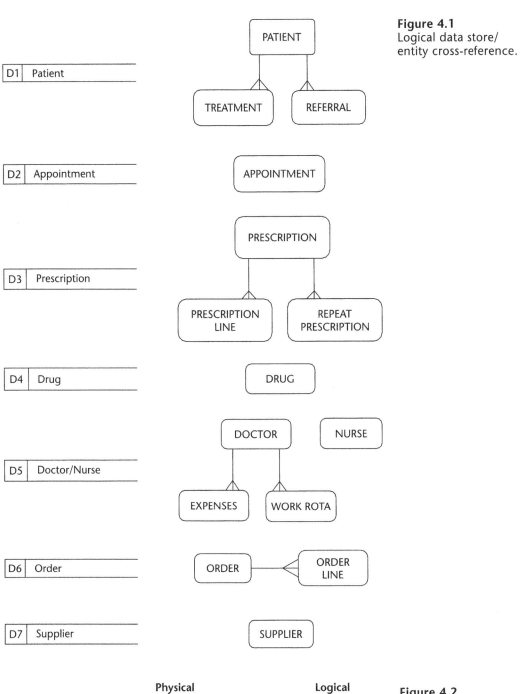

Figure 4.1
Logical data store/
entity cross-reference.

D1	Patient
D2	Appointment
D3	Prescription
D4	Drug
D5	Doctor/Nurse
D6	Order
D7	Supplier

Physical

| 1.3 | Reception |

Add patient to
Doctors' list and
Patient records

Logical

| 1.3 | |

Create new patient

Figure 4.2
Converting a physical
process to a logical
one.

If we put all these simple steps into practice, we will produce a set of current logical DFDs. These are shown in Figures 4.3–4.7. These might usefully be compared to the current physical DFDs at the end of Chapter 2 (Figures 2.16–2.20).

In Figure 4.3, note that processes 1.1 'File student list' and 1.2 'Process registration form' have been merged to produce the logical process 'Register patient'. This could have been called 'Create patient', but the use of the word 'register' is more descriptive of what actually happens.

Figure 4.3
Current logical DFD – 'Register patient'.

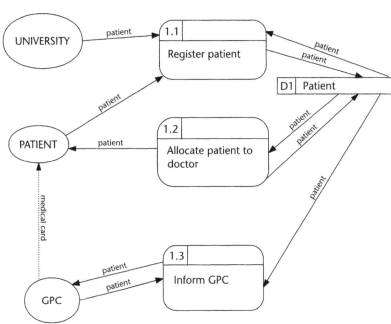

All of the data stores used by these processes have been logically grouped into one data store, 'Patient', and, similarly, the data flows are all concerned with 'patient'. Even a data flow such as 'doctor's name', which might appear to be about the doctor, is logically about the patient. The name of the doctor would appear in the 'Patient' entity rather than the 'Doctor', as can be seen from the entity model.

The logical DFDs normally seem much simpler than the physical ones. This is because many of the constraints and unnecessary activities have been taken away, leaving the bare bones of what happens.

Figure 4.4 shows the 'Process appointments' DFD in logical form. The physical processes 'Take appointment request' and 'Create new appointment' have been deemed to be part of the same logical process which we call 'Create new appointment'.

'Process Patient Requirements' has been converted into logical format in Figure 4.5.

The only significant change here is that a new data flow has been added. This is 'prescription', which goes to the Prescription Monitoring Authority. Previously, this was done in a separate process – 4.4 'Compile PMA report'.

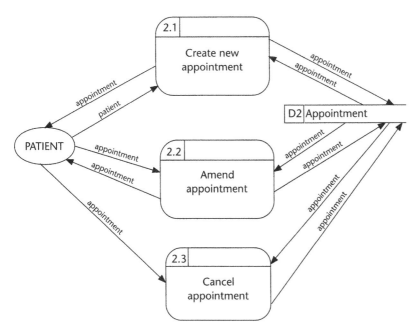

Figure 4.4
Current logical DFD –
'Process
appointments'.

However, logically the prescription information should go directly to the PMA as part of 3.3 'Prescribe treatment'. How this might happen is not a consideration as yet, and it may be that we still end up compiling a separate report.

Things get a little more complex in process 4 – 'Process Management Information'. The timesheet is not a logical entity: it is a physical entity, a form. Or rather a scrappy bit of paper that Nurse Payne thrusts under the noses of the receptionists at regular intervals in an effort to get them to fill in their actual working hours. It is not part of our entity model. Essentially, the information contained in it appears in the 'Work Rota' entity. As a result, the rota appears on our logical DFDs and not the timesheet.

It should also be remembered that the 'Work Rota' entity has been placed in D5 'Doctor/Nurse' for the sake of convenience.

Process 4.3 'Process staff income/expenses' was the only process to be taken down to a level 3 DFD as part of the current physical DFDs. This was done because it was too complex to be completely clear as a level 2 process. The level 3 DFD was given in Figure 2.20 (p. 32).

Many of the processes in this DFD have been discussed above. We have already decided that 4.3.3 'Post pay claim' and 4.3.4 'Receive pay slips' can be removed because they refer to physical, not logical, activities. Similarly, 4.3.1 'Check timesheets' adds nothing and can be seen as part of 4.3.2 'Compile pay claim'. As a result, we are left with only two logical processes. It is therefore no longer necessary to have a lower level DFD and we can incorporate these processes in their level 1 process – 4.3 'Update staff income/expenses'; see Figure 4.6.

Processes 4.4 and 4.5 on the physical DFD involve compiling reports. We have already seen how the PMA report can be removed by adding a data flow to the PMA in Figure 4.5. Similarly, we can remove the process of

Figure 4.5
Current logical DFD –
'Process Patient
Requirements'.

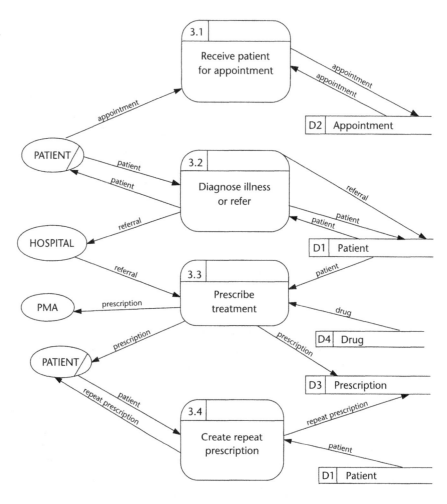

gathering data for the accountant in 4.4 by adding data flows to the accountant in the logical DFDs.

A final point is that there is no logical reason why pay information should be part of our system at all. The GPC pays the doctors, so logically the data flow is between these two entities. How this might happen in practice remains to be considered, like many things.

The final logical DFD concerns physical process 5 – 'Maintain supplies' (Figure 4.7).

As mentioned above, we should show financial data such as orders, invoices and payments going directly to the accountant, not going into physical processes like compiling reports. Otherwise this DFD is straightforward.

The logical DFDs are now complete. We have seen how several of the problems, many of which are related to the 'Betty and George' way of doing things, have now disappeared. However, some problems still remain and it is time to consider the Requirements Catalogue in detail to consider how we might resolve the outstanding problems.

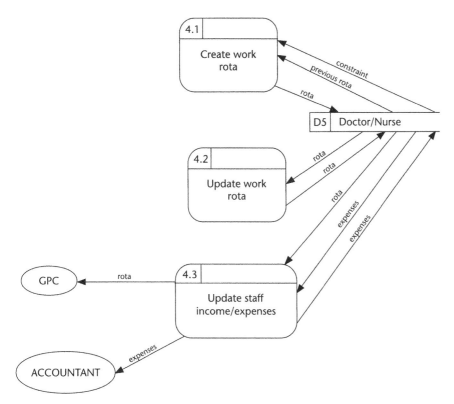

Figure 4.6
Current logical DFD –
'Update staff income/
expenses'.

4.3 | Logicalization at Swillbuckets

The data store/entity cross-reference and the current logical DFDs for Swillbuckets are provided in Figures 4.8–4.13.

The cross-reference in Figure 4.8 does highlight the issue of whether FOOD ORDER and DRINK ORDER should be separate entities, or whether it would be more sensible to combine them into an ORDER entity. We will consider this in our Problem and Requirements Catalogue.

The DFD of Figure 4.9 is very straightforward, but that in Figure 4.10 – 'Book artistes' – raises an issue.

The very title of the process indicates that there should be a BOOKING entity in our system. The presence of the 'booking form' data flow reinforces this view. However, currently Jack does not need this as he stores this booking information within the EVENT entity. This is fine as long as there is only one artiste appearing at the event. But if we start booking more than one artiste per event, we will soon hit problems. So it may well be that a requirement for our new system would be the facility to book more than one artiste per event. Jack's initial reaction to this idea is lukewarm:

> We once had Jade Green and her Dancing Chihuahuas on with Leapy Len's Flea Circus. A disaster. Half the members wear insect repellent to this day. I vowed then that it would be one act per night. They're bad enough on their own, but two together is asking for trouble.

Figure 4.7
Current logical DFD –
'Maintain supplies'.

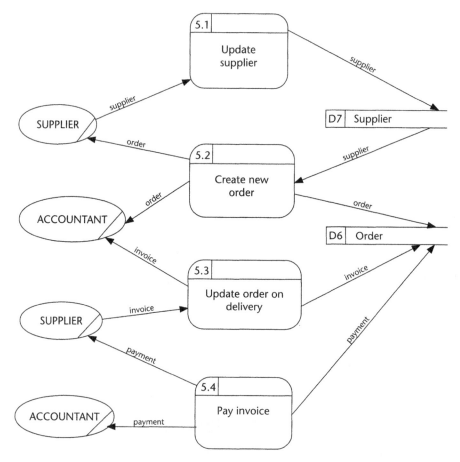

Nevertheless, we could build in the facility quite easily in case Jack changes his mind.

The next process at Swillbuckets, 'Order Drinks and Supplies' (Figure 4.11), also throws up an issue.

Whilst we have a DISH entity to record information about the food side of the Club, there is no method for recording drinks information. In terms of stock, Jack tends to adopt the 'scraping the barrel' approach. He does not order more beer until even the frantic pumping of the bar staff fails to persuade any more liquid to issue from the beer taps. This has been known to cause a degree of concern among members eager for another pint (or eight). Indeed, it was Nick Coal's verbal invective which persuaded Jack of the need for change.

So the new system must record drink stock levels very carefully in order that Jack does not have to have Nick's pint glass surgically removed.

The next process – 'Process payments' is simple enough to convert to logical form (Figure 4.12).

However, its simplicity indicates that we may be able to dispense with it. For example, we could move 4.1 'Pay supplier' into the 'Order drinks and supplies' DFD, making it process 3.4. Similarly, 4.2 'Pay artiste' could go

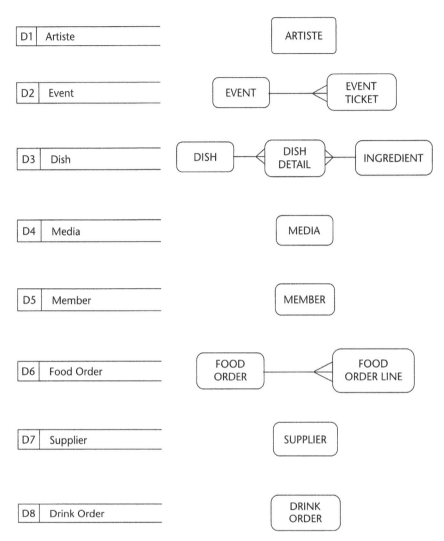

Figure 4.8
Data store/entity
cross-reference
(Swillbuckets).

into the 'Book artistes' DFD, making it process 2.4. This would allow us to remove the top-level process 'Process payments' from our top-level current logical DFD. This change will be made in the required logical DFDs.

The 'Manage events' process is shown in logical form (Figure 4.13) to complete the current logical DFDs for Swillbuckets.

4.4 Problem and requirements catalogue

This catalogue is a constantly changing document. It is created when the analyst first interviews users and is added to at various points during the systems analysis. After the completion of the logical DFDs, it is a sensible time to consider the current position.

Problems can be defined as:

● things the system is not doing correctly

Figure 4.9
Current logical DFD –
'Process
membership'.

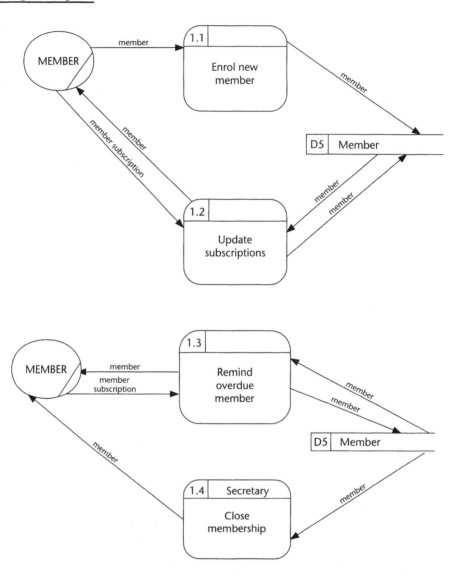

- things the system is doing inefficiently/ineffectively
- things the system should do but is failing to do

  Requirements are requested features of the new system.

4.4.1 The Medical Centre

As we saw in Section 2.3.1, a useful template for recording problems and requirements might be something like the one in Figure 2.2.

It is now time to develop a set of problems and requirements, agree them with the user and start to consider priorities. We will, of course, need to come back to the Catalogue at a later stage.

We have already seen the one in Figure 4.14.

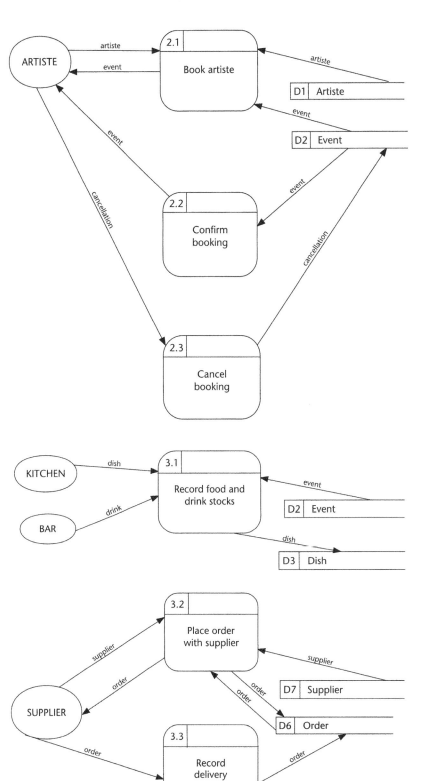

Figure 4.10
Current logical DFD –
'Book artistes'.

Figure 4.11
Current logical DFD –
'Order drinks and
supplies'.

Figure 4.12
Current logical DFD –
'Process payments'.

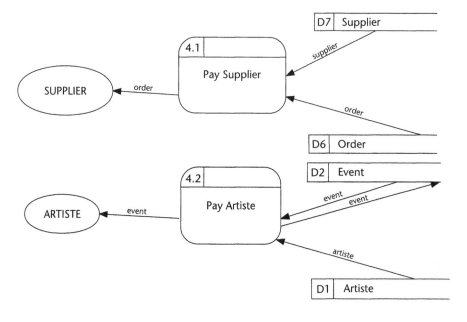

Figure 4.13
Current logical DFD –
'Manage events'.

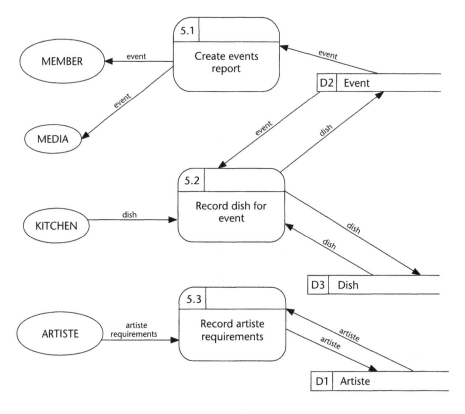

Problems/requirements catalogue

System: Medical Centre
Author: Kevin Bowman

Date: 30/10/03	Page 1 of 1	Draft/~~final~~

P/R P	No: 1	Source: Betty	Priority: 1

Description:
Double booking is occurring as a result of the Appointments Book being hard to maintain accurately.

Benefits if action taken:
No more arguments with Amanda Stote. Patients seen on time. Fewer complaints.

Comments/suggested solutions:
Computerised Appointments Data Entry Form to include Patients combo box and pre-formatted appointment slots.

Related probs/reqts/documents:
Requirement 1
DFD Appointments

Figure 4.14
Requirements
Catalogue P1.

Here is a summary of all the problems and requirements in bullet form:

● Double booking occurring due to the Appointments Book being hard to maintain and Betty being past her best (Figure 4.14) (Ref: P1).

– Suggested solution: Figure 4.14.

● Repeat appointments being missed because staff have no time, or indeed inclination, to remind patients of their appointments (Ref: P2).

– Suggested solution: an automatic mailing system so that when a repeat prescription is made, a letter is printed off at the appropriate time.

● Patient records being difficult to locate, especially when the cat has had them (Ref: P3).

– Suggested solution: records securely stored in a database system.

● Patient details being incorrectly entered – there is no blood group P, for example (Ref: P4).

- Suggested solution: validation and verification checks set up to help data entry.

● Prescriptions are normally illegible – Chris Longbottom was recently almost given boot polish instead of boil poultice, which might have had irreversible consequences (Ref: P5).

- Suggested solution: a prescription printing facility for each doctor – these can be signed and a record stored for the PMA.

● Nurse Payne being worn down with all the financial information required by the accountant – even syringing wax from ears is stimulating in comparison (Ref: P6).

- Suggested solution: financial data might be entered into a database or spreadsheet system. This file could be sent to the accountant regularly. Alternatively, a web-based system could be set up whereby the accountant has access to the database online.

● It would be sensible and unbelievably lucrative to negotiate a deal with pharmaceutical companies keen for the doctors to prescribe their drugs. The Centre would need to process prescription information so that the Nurse could check that the Centre is receiving the correct amount of money.

- Suggested solution: prescription information is stored and payment calculated on the basis of agreements with pharmaceutical companies.

Key requirements are:

● An effective appointments system (Ref: R1)

● A fast and effective way of storing and retrieving patient records (Ref: R2)

● A quicker way of producing legible prescriptions (Ref: R3)

● A report showing the work schedules of each member of staff (Ref: R4)

● A report to the GPC, detailing the patient processing for each month (Ref: R5)

● A report to the PMA, detailing the drugs prescribed for that month (Ref: R6)

● A system for Nurse Payne to keep track of orders and store financial information (Ref: R7)

Slightly less pressing are:

● Fast information concerning the catchment area for the Centre (Ref: R8)

● Up to date information about the latest medical techniques – Dr McLean still uses leeches (Ref: R9)

● Information about referrals to hospitals – diagnosis, treatment etc. – which is then added to patient records (Ref: R10)

Stop press: the Prescriptions Monitoring Agency have just been on the phone to George. Apparently they want a full report each month from now on, as some questionable prescribing practices have been noted. It will no longer be sufficient just to send the raw data to them. The exact details of the required report were lost in translation as George seemed to lose the power of speech when recounting the conversation. However, they will send a full description in the post.

4.4.2 The problem and requirements catalogue for Swillbuckets

Artiste booking information is currently stuffed into the Events folder. This would confuse our new computer system. It has already confused Jack. Last week, a few elderly stalwarts were quietly waiting for the Gypsy Ky-Lee Clairvoyant's show to commence, when Rocky Rocket and the Rockettes burst onto the stage like a howitzer. Mr Popplewell couldn't keep down solids for days afterwards.

- It would be better all round if there was a way of storing booking information more effectively (Ref: P1).

  – Suggested solution: a new BOOKING entity.

- Supplier and order information is all stored in the Supplier shoebox (if it's ever stored at all). One more order and the whole box could explode (Ref: P2).

  – Suggested solution: Supplies and Order information stored separately but linked together.

- Members' subscriptions become due at different times of the year and Jack can't keep track. Even the robust interventions of Amanda Stote don't always persuade members to renew their subscriptions on time. If Amanda had up-to-date and accurate information, however, at least she would be sure to pin the correct person up against the pool table (Ref: P3).

  – Suggested solution: a regular report which lists overdue members and a mail merge facility to print reminders before the subscription becomes overdue.

- Jack needs up to date drink stock information so that he can order more barrels in good time (Ref: P4).

  – Suggested solution: a new DRINK entity with stock information within it. It is worth considering combining the FOOD ORDER and DRINK ORDER entities into one entity called ORDER. However, since Jack only ever orders drinks from one SUPPLIER, DRINK ORDER has a different relationship with SUPPLIER than FOOD ORDER. In the future, though, Jack may order from a number of suppliers, so we need to allow for this in our design. For the time being we will keep them separate, as this is more flexible.

- Jack recently had a phone call from Lard, of 'Little and Lard' claiming that they had not been paid for their last 'performance'. Jack informed Lard that they had drunk their fee after, and indeed during, their act. Lard claimed that he had no memory of this fiscal arrangement. Jack said this wasn't surprising. Threats were made and the upshot is that Jack has reluctantly decided to put a cheque in the post. If Jack had proper payment records, this unsavoury incident might have been avoided. Jack might not have been left with the damaging mental image of 150 kg of Lard bearing down on him (Ref: P5).

  - Suggested solution: add payment information into the new BOOKING entity.

- The 'Forthcoming Events List' is time-consuming to produce, especially as Jack has to start from a blank page every time (Ref: P6).

  - Suggested solution: a word processor or DTP template which could be linked to a database to produce the list automatically. Alternatively, the information could be dynamically displayed on a web site. However, since most of the Swillbuckets members think the World Wide Web is another name for the Inland Revenue, this is probably a non-starter. However, an email link for the media might be appropriate.

Key requirements are:

- A new booking system
- A new supplies and ordering system
- An overdue members report
- Accurate drink stock information
- A record of payments made to artistes and suppliers
- A better way of producing and disseminating the events list

Slightly less pressing are:

- Better supplier information
- Some feedback on members' likes and dislikes – a record of which members attend which events might be a start
- The flexibility to book more than one artiste per event – on the understanding that animal life will only feature in one act

Summary

In this chapter, we have looked at data flow modelling techniques to model what the current system does. We have also started to consider what requirements the user has for the new system. We have now completed our investigation of the current system and can now begin to consider the new system and what options are available to us.

Exercises

4.1 Logicalize the following, *if necessary*:

● Type and copy invoice

● Collate customer details

● SR1 form – blue

● File details from new customer

● View patient's name and address

● Photocopy application form

● Delivery note

4.2 Logicalize the mail order book company DFD shown in Figure 4.15 (overleaf).

Figure 4.15
Book company DFD.

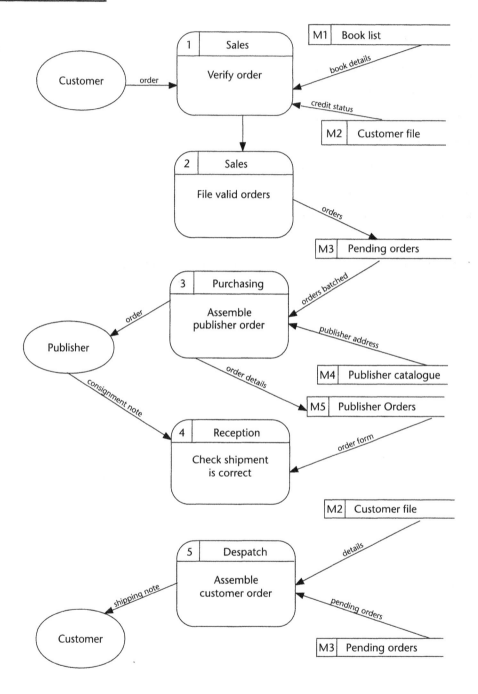

CHAPTER 5

Business system options

5.1 ▌ Business system options

Creating the Business System Options (BSOs) and then selecting one of them constitutes the second Stage of SSADM. It is here that we begin to move away from analysis and into design. Nevertheless, we may well continue to identify problems and requirements as we progress, so, in a sense, analysis never finishes. What we do not want to do is find lots of problems as we near the end of the system life cycle, as these may prove impossible, or very expensive, to resolve.

We should also try not to simply provide a more efficient version of the old system. We should consider quite revolutionary changes. It may be that turning Swillbuckets into a bingo hall is the best thing for everyone. It will be the user that makes the final decision about which direction to take.

Normally, the business system options consist of five or six preferred options for the new system. They will all be based on the Problem and Requirements Catalogue primarily, but will take different approaches to meeting the needs of the organization. A group consisting of, for example, users and analysts will meet to define the options. Each option will need to be described and modelled. The modelling takes the form of a Required Logical DFD for each option. These options are normally presented to management, or a senior user, to whittle them down and make a choice. The final choice may well not be one of the original options, but a mixture of two or three of them.

5.2 ▌ Simple steps in creating business system options

1   Assemble the inputs to the process.

The inputs are the logical DFDs, the entity model and the Problem and Requirements Catalogue.

2 Assemble the team who will create the BSOs.
This will normally be the analyst and one or more users.

3 Consider the aims of the organization and business plans.
Any decisions taken about the information systems in an organization must be in keeping with the aims and strategies of that organization. If a business plan exists, it will provide guidelines for the budget for the new system. This kind of information is vital, as budget and time-scale will be key parameters in the production and consideration of the BSOs.

4 The BSO production team produce a range of ideas.
To begin with, the team should aim to be as creative as possible within the constraints imposed by the organization.

5 Five or six BSOs are agreed for further discussion or presentation.
The production team decide upon five or six options which will be discussed with management or senior users. These may range from a cheap option to an expensive option. One option might resolve all the problems in the Problem and Requirements Catalogue, whereas another might only deal with the top-priority problems. The BSOs may consider alternatives, such as centralizing an organization's information systems or making them more locally autonomous. There may be various networking and communications options to consider.

6 Two or three options are selected for detailed analysis.
The analyst must investigate the implications of the chosen options very carefully. Required Logical DFDs should be drawn up for each option. A cost–benefit analysis will be required which must consider the impact of the proposed changes on the organization. There may be a need to produce an entity model for each option.

7 A choice is made and documented.
Management makes a choice and the chosen option is described. It may be a mixture of two or three of the options. This specification of the required system now forms the basis of further development.

8 Elementary process descriptions are produced.
These are brief narrative descriptions of the processes in the required logical DFDs. If there are any lower level DFDs, then these must be described rather than their higher level equivalent. These descriptions will form the basis of the programs required to make the system work.

5.3 BSOs at the Medical Centre

Each of our BSOs must address all the key problems and requirements, but may address all, some or none of the less pressing concerns.

The BSO production team might consist of a receptionist, a doctor, the Nurse, a GPC representative and the analyst. After discussions, the following options might be arrived at:

Option 1   A fully networked database system with an online supplies ordering system, email facilities and a printer in every surgery.

Option 2   A networked database system with a terminal and printer in every surgery and in reception, with Internet access and email.

Option 3   A simple network with a printer in reception only.

Option 4   A stand alone system.

Option 5   Keep the manual system, but get reliable staff to administer it.

Option 6   A radical option involving the closing down of the Centre in its current form and replacing it with a phone-in diagnostics service and a drug dispenser.

After extensive discussions, it is decided that Option 1 is too expensive and far too modern for the medical profession to consider. Option 6, although favoured by the GPC, is rejected on the grounds that the staff would be unemployable elsewhere. Option 5 is rejected as the notion of 'reliable staff' is felt to be unrealistic. Option 4 is also rejected as there would soon be several different versions of patient records on the different PCs.

So we come down to Option 2 or 3. We should now create Required Logical DFDs for each of these options and produce a cost–benefit analysis. In this case, however, the DFDs would be almost identical, as we would still be doing the same processes. The difference is that Option 2 would allow process 3.3 'Prescribe treatment' to be performed more efficiently than Option 3. This is because the prescription could be printed during the appointment with the doctor rather than having to collect it afterwards from reception. An additional benefit of Option 2 would be that the doctor would have the benefit of online medical information to help with diagnosis. The required logical DFD for patient processing would look like Figure 5.1.

This is almost identical to the current logical DFD (Figure 4.5). Indeed, none of the requirements in the Problems and Requirements Catalogue would require us to alter the current logical DFDs very much in order to turn them into required logical DFDs. The only important change would be the introduction of a new process to produce the report now required by the PMA. The other requirements are simply a matter of improving and automating the processes on the current logical DFDs.

The cost–benefit analysis might look like the following.

Option 2: Fully networked database system with internet access

This involves networking the Medical Centre with terminals in reception, and in each doctor's and the nurse's surgeries. All terminals would have Internet access. Additionally, an integrated database system would be available incorporating appointments, registration, patient records, prescriptions

Figure 5.1
Required Logical DFD
'Process patient
requirements'
(Option 2).

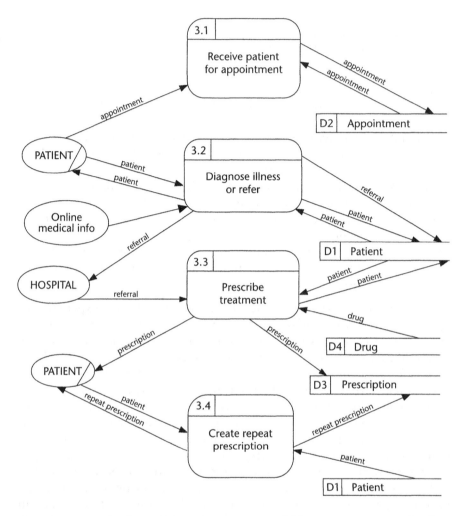

and management information. The nurse would have access to a supplies system.

A Required Physical DFD could be drawn demonstrating the effects. This would show whether the processes are computerized or not, batch or online, and where they are done.

Costs
Costs would be quite high – a server PC plus at least five terminals, five printers, communications hardware and software, other software, ISP costs, additional phone charges etc.

Approximate cost: £50,000.

Benefits
Benefits would be impressive:

● Automatically produce a range of management information reports which could save lots of money eventually.

- Might need fewer staff (sorry George).

- All doctors would have immediate access to all patient records.

- Even Betty would not be able to double book appointments, as the system would prevent this happening.

- Easy access to important online medical information would improve diagnosis and might save hundreds of lives (a week).

- Security features would prevent unauthorized access to private information. Of course this wouldn't stop Chelsea gossiping.

- Validation checks would ensure that only sensible information is entered – more or less.

- Printing prescriptions would allow chemists to read them instead of having to phone up the Centre and ask what they said.

- Repeat appointments could be automatically entered into the system and letters reminding patients could be printed.

To be useful, the analysis of benefits needs to have some sort of figure or rating attached to it. This might be an assessment of the financial benefits of the option under scrutiny, or it might be a risk assessment resulting in a risk rating.

Time
It is estimated that this option would take 4 months to deliver.

Impact
This would have a major effect on the quality of the service, but would have implications for staff training. The phrase, 'Betty, connect the tape streamer and start the backup' is not one which could be uttered with much conviction.

A similar analysis would need to be carried out for the remaining options and then a final decision reached. Let's assume Option 2 is chosen.

5.4 | BSOs at Swillbuckets

After due consideration of the options with Amanda, Freddo and someone in the bar, Jack has chosen a database system containing the required information on bookings, orders, suppliers and members. Jack has decided not to try to gather information on which members attend which events, as he feels that would be overkill. As a result, the MEMBER entity will not be linked to the rest of the system on our required entity model. We will still store information about members, but not about which events they attend.

In a surprise move, Jack has decided to go for a web site. This is an amazing turnaround. When first asked if he wanted to go online, Jack thought he was being invited on a fishing trip. However, he was quick to see the benefits of a web site containing forthcoming events information. This could be linked to the database and would automatically display the events as Jack entered them. This would save him having to phone the media, as the local newshounds could simply log into Jack's web site for information. His flier for the members could be generated from the database and printed as a report.

A small network would be required linking Jack's PC in the office behind the bar with Freddo's PC in the corner of the kitchen by the freezer. This would enable Freddo to keep the food stock and dish information up to date.

Costs
Two PCs (one a server), one printer, communications hardware and software, web access, a couple of swivel chairs – about £10,000. Running costs might be £50 a month.

Benefits
Jack would save a lot of time currently spent leafing through shoeboxes looking for records. With all this spare time, he is thinking of joining the Gnarlsborough Marrow Growing Circle in an attempt to meet some interesting people and/or vegetables.

The sharing of information between Jack and Freddo would be of immense benefit to the whole community. Never again would Jack buy a gross of pigs' trotters, throw them in the corner of the kitchen and find Freddo boiling them up six weeks later. With the new system, Freddo would know as soon as Jack made a purchase and could plan his dishes accordingly. He *could* do this, though he might not bother.

Up-to-date drink information would save Jack from running out of key drinks such as Black Rock Stout, Dark Ramshead Bitter, Old Moor Porter and Babycham. This should increase sales, improve customer satisfaction, and generally make members very happy right up to the point when consciousness is temporarily lost.

Freddo is keen to put his meat recipes up on the web site. He is confident a book deal might be in the offing. He hasn't quite decided on a title, though *A Love Affair with Offal* is the current favourite.

Time
It is expected that the system could be up and running in two to three months.

Impact
As long as Jack and Freddo keep the information up to date, the impact should be considerable in terms of efficiency gains. However, there is a clear danger that the PCs will just gather dust after an initial burst of enthusiasm. It is important, therefore, that both Jack and Freddo feel closely involved in all aspects of the design. This will make them more likely to use the system.

Summary

In this chapter, we have considered the range of business options available in our case studies and how to choose a preferred option. This completes Stage 2 of SSADM.

CHAPTER 6

Requirements specification

6.1 | Requirements specification

We know, broadly speaking, the kind of system we are working towards. We now need to specify it. To specify it means to model and describe it in detail. This will require the analyst to produce a full set of required logical DFDs, a required entity model and a sensible data structure. Various checks will also be required to ensure that we haven't missed anything.

6.2 | Required logical models

We must now produce a top-level required logical DFD, any lower level DFDs which might be required and a required entity model.

The top-level required logical DFD for the Medical Centre might look like Figure 6.1.

Figure 6.2 shows the required logical DFD Level 2 for 'Process management information'.

The required logical DFD for 'Process patient requirements' has already been completed (Figure 5.1). The other Level 2 required logical DFDs are identical to the current logical DFDs, as discussed in the previous chapter.

The required entity model would need to reflect the new entities DRUG COMPANY and PAYMENT. We would also need to calculate and store the expected payment somewhere. This could be done by extending the PRESCRIPTION LINE, DRUG and DRUG COMPANY entities, so that the system calculates the payment generated by each prescription. Exactly how this calculation is made will be looked at in the next chapter. The new entity PAYMENT will be required to store the details of payments from the drug companies. A further decision is to merge the DOCTOR and NURSE entities, since NURSE would only have one record. This makes it untenable as an entity.

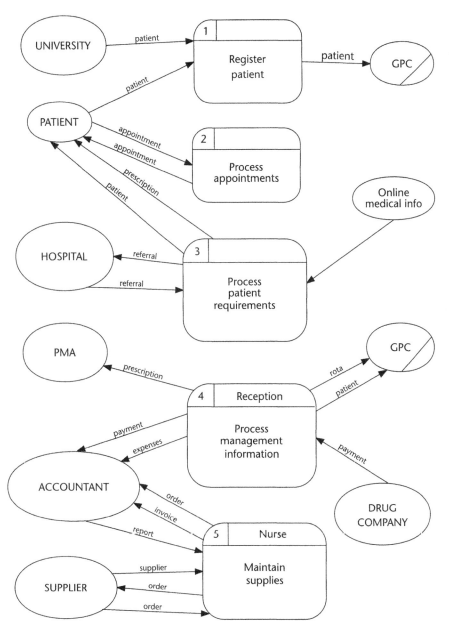

Figure 6.1
Required logical DFD
– Level 1.

The required entity model is shown in Figure 6.3. Note that the company name in DRUG is referred to as 'Supplier'. The attribute 'Supplier' is, therefore, an alias for DCompanyName. This means that the attributes are identical but have two different names.

The required entity model for Swillbuckets Club also needs creating. The BOOKING entity has been inserted and the EVENT TICKET and MEDIA entities removed, as Jack does not wish to gather information about these entities. DRINK and DRINK ORDER LINE have been inserted to allow for more accurate drink stock information.

Figure 6.2
Required logical DFD
'Process management
information'.

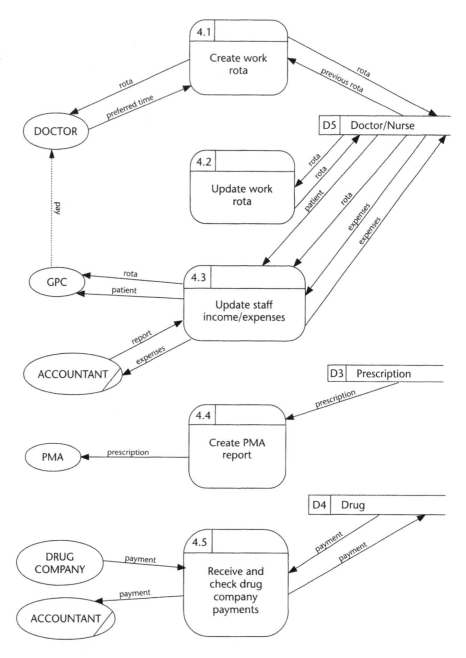

6.3 Elementary process descriptions

These provide descriptions of the lowest level (elementary) processes for
the required system. The format for these can vary depending upon the
nature of the process being described. Some processes are very simple
and will just require a short written description. For example, process
2.3 'Cancel Appointment' is simply a matter of finding the particular

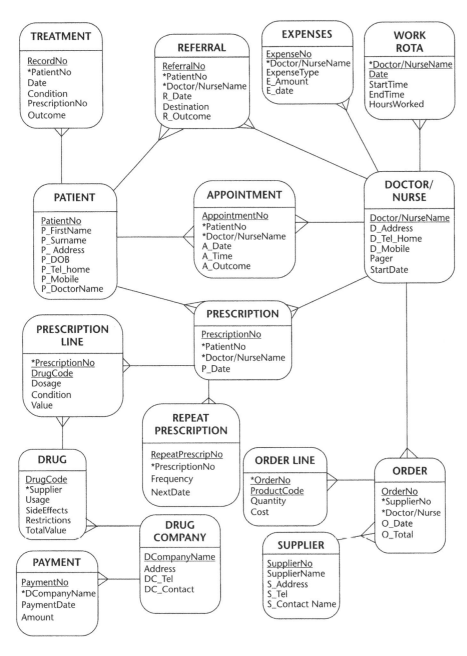

Figure 6.3
Required entity
model – Medical
Centre.

appointment and deleting it from the system. Process 2.1 'Create new Appointment' is fairly straightforward and might look like Table 6.1.

However, the process 1.1 'Register Patient' is a little more complex. We need to find out if patients are eligible to be registered by ensuring they are either a student or living in the catchment area. If they are eligible, we need to register them and allocate them to a doctor. We need a policy for doing

Figure 6.4
Required entity
model – Swillbuckets.

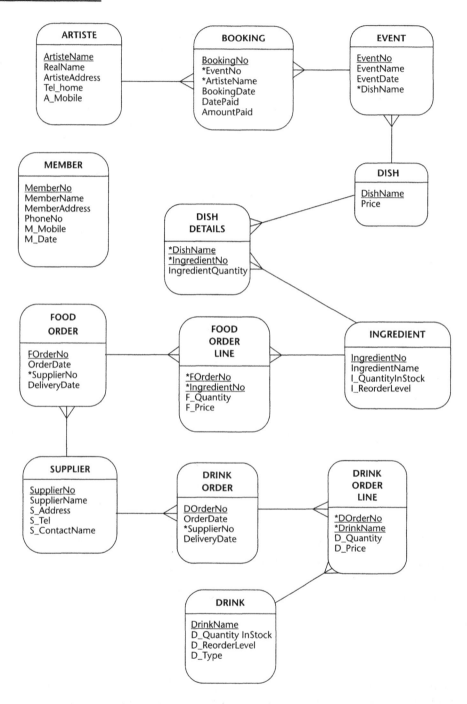

this. It may be that we simply allocate them to the doctor with the lowest number of patients.

All of this is a little complex to write in narrative form and could lead to confusion. It is a good idea, in cases like this, to use techniques such as structured English or decision trees.

Table 6.1 *Elementary process description example.*

Elementary Process Description		
System: Medical Centre		
Author: Kevin Bowman		
Date: 30/3/03	**Page** 1 of 1	**Draft**/~~Final~~
Process Id: 2.1		
Process Name: Create new appointment		
Inputs to Process: Notification of Patient's need for appointment, preferred times		**Outputs from Process:** Appointment created, Patient informed
Process Description: Patient requests appointment. Receptionist checks which appointments are available. The patient is given some options for an appointment and chooses the preferred time. The appointment is created and confirmed with the patient.		

6.3.1 Structured English and decision trees

Structured English is sometimes referred to as pseudo-code and is a kind of half-way house between English and a programming language. It makes use of some conventions originally used in languages such as Pascal or BASIC. Commands such as IF... ENDIF or REPEAT ... UNTIL can be used. However, the syntax does not have to conform to a rigid programming language and spoken English words can be used as well.

Using structured English, we might come up with something like this for 1.1 'Register Patient':

```
IF patient NOT registered
   IF patient is a student
      register patient
   ELSE
      IF patient in catchment area
         register patient
      ELSE
         send patient elsewhere
      ENDIF
   ENDIF
ELSE
   inform patient they are registered already
ENDIF
```

Of course this is just a rough description of the process, but it does give the poor programmer, who will eventually have to implement our system, a pretty clear idea of what is required.

A decision tree modelling the same process would look like Figure 6.5.

Figure 6.5
A decision tree for
process 1.1 'Register
patient'.

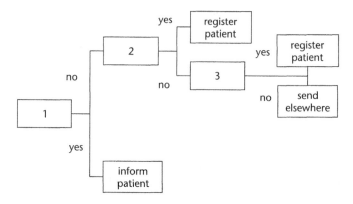

1 Is patient registered?
2 Is patient a student?
3 Is patient in catchment area?

Clearly, this technique models only the decision-making aspects in a process. It does not model the whole process as fully as the structured English example.

It must be remembered that we are still in the early stages of design and these processes could change further. When we are a little more certain of what is required for the new system, we will use a further, more definitive, technique for describing processes called decision tables.

6.3.2 Decision tables

Decision tables are an alternative to structured English and decision trees and offer a more detailed specification. They are only necessary when there is the possibility of confusion concerning the exact logic of a particular process.

A decision table is made up of four sections:

1 The possible conditions which might apply to the process.

2 The possible actions to take.

3 The possible combination of conditions which can occur.

4 The choice of action for each possible combination of conditions.

As an example, we will look at the process at the Medical Centre – '3.5 Receive and Check Discount'.

The drug companies operate a scheme whereby they categorize a surgery as gold, silver or bronze each month, depending upon the value of their drugs prescribed by the surgery. If the surgery prescribes over £50,000 worth of drugs in a month, they become a gold surgery and receive a payment worth 10% of the value of the drugs. If they prescribe £10,000–£50,000 worth of drugs, they are categorized as silver and receive 5% of the value. If they prescribe less than £10,000 worth of drugs, they receive bronze status which entitles them to a free first-aid kit, unless they received a first-aid kit last month, in which case they receive nothing.

In our new system, it will be the responsibility of Nurse Payne to check that payments are accurate. Nurse Payne is not keen on financial administration, however, and we need to make this process as automatic as possible. Using a decision table, we can specify a computer program to check the payments automatically. All Nurse Payne will need to do is compare the payment expected with the payment received.

So let's set up the decision table using simple steps.

6.3.3 Simple steps in decision tables

1 List the possible conditions.
The possible conditions for this process are:

Condition 1: Prescribed more than £50,000 worth of drugs (>50)
Condition 2: Prescribed £10,000–£50,000 worth of drugs (10–50)
Condition 3: Prescribed less than £10,000 worth of drugs (<10)
Condition 4: Received first-aid kit last month

There must be no ambiguity here. For example, it must be clear what happens if exactly £50,000 worth of drugs is prescribed. In this case, it would meet Condition 2 only.

2 List the possible actions.
The possible actions are:

Action 1: Gold status (10% payment)
Action 2: Silver status (5% payment)
Action 3: Bronze status (first-aid kit)
Action 4: Receive nothing

3 Calculate how many combinations of conditions can occur.
This calculation is performed using the simple expression 2^c. In other words, if there are four conditions, there will be 2^4 combinations of conditions i.e. 16 conditions. These normally take the form of a Y (Yes) or a N (No) sequence in the table (see Figure 6.6).

4 Prescribe actions for each combination of conditions.
These are prescribed by the conditions laid down above.

5 Draw the draft table.
The table is drawn using a four-part grid as in Figure 6.6.

There is a technique to ensure that all possible combinations of 'Y's and 'N's are covered. We know there are 16 combinations of conditions. In the first row (>50,000), we make the first 8 'Y's and the second 8 'N's. In the next row (10,000–50,000), we put 4 'Y's followed by 4 'N's and alternate in patterns of 4. In the next row (<10,000), we alternate in patterns of 2.

Figure 6.6
Draft decision table.

>50,000	Y	Y	Y	Y	Y	Y	Y	Y	N	N	N	N	N	N	N	N
10,000–50,000	Y	Y	Y	Y	N	N	N	N	Y	Y	Y	Y	N	N	N	N
<10,000	Y	Y	N	N	Y	Y	N	N	Y	Y	N	N	Y	Y	N	N
First-aid kit last month	Y	N	Y	N	Y	N	Y	N	Y	N	Y	N	Y	N	Y	N
10% payment	X	X	X	X	X	X	X	X								
5% payment									X	X	X	X				
First-aid kit													X		X	
No payment														X		X

Finally, in the last row (First-aid kit), we alternate every time. This ensures that if we read vertically down the columns, every possible combination occurs somewhere.

6   Rationalize the table.
This involves removing the impossible conditions and editing the redundant conditions. An example of an impossible condition is: if the drugs are worth over £50,000, then they can't also be worth £10,000–£50,000, or less than £50,000, so these columns can be removed. The first column in Figure 6.6 is just such a column. Similarly, it cannot be the case that none of the conditions applies, so the column with all 'N's can be removed.

A redundant condition occurs if the same action applies whether a condition is 'Y' or 'N'. In this circumstance we place a dashed line in the condition entry. For example, whether the Medical Centre received a first-aid kit last month is irrelevant if prescriptions are over £10,000. The Centre still receives the payment.

The rationalized table (Figure 6.7) looks much simpler.

Figure 6.7
Rationalized decision table.

>50,000	Y	N	N	N
10,000–50,000	N	Y	N	N
<10,000	N	N	Y	Y
First-aid kit last month	-	-	N	Y
10% payment	X			
5% payment		X		
First-aid kit			X	
No payment				X

The decision table could now form the basis of a program to implement a routine to calculate the payment for each drug prescribed and output a report each month for the Nurse to check against actual payments. The

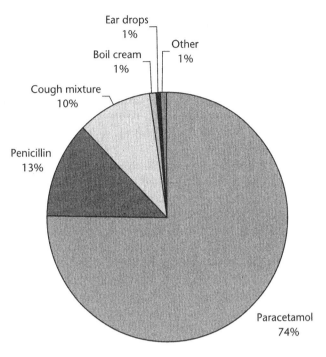

Ear drops
1%

Boil cream
1%

Other
1%

Cough mixture
10%

Penicillin
13%

Paracetamol
74%

Figure 6.8
Prescription values.

report could even contain a chart to inform the doctors, which might look like Figure 6.8.

6.4 ▌ Input/output design

This part of the process is crucial to the success or failure of the system. If users do not input data correctly, we will not have an effective system. Readers will, no doubt, be familiar with the maxim 'Garbage in, garbage out'; it is at this stage that we can do most to avoid the garbage going in. Incidentally, the maxim above also happens to be Freddo Smitho's motto on dish production, but let's not dwell on that.

Any system, computerized or not, can be stripped down to three basic components: INPUT, PROCESSING and OUTPUT. Well, here we are going to design two of the three. We need to do everything we can to ensure that the user only inputs sensible, accurate data. We also need to ensure that outputs are easy to understand and relevant to the user. They are, after all, the reason for the system being created.

Screen designs are the first impression the users will get of the system, and as such the system may be judged on the basis of these screens. If the users do not like these screens, for whatever reason, they may turn against the system and possibly not use it at all.

Strangely, we need to consider the outputs before we can consider the inputs. This is because we need to identify what outputs are required, before we can be sure what inputs will be needed to produce these outputs.

6.4.1 Output design

So what is an output? An output might be a printed report for a manager or external body. Alternatively, an output might be a screen displaying the quantity of drinks in stock or a chart showing the number of patients each doctor has registered. Management reports can be of various types: detailed or just a summary. So outputs come in many shapes and sizes. The analyst will need to decide which type of output is required in each case and to document this.

The outputs can be identified from the required logical DFDs. Any data flows to external entities are outputs. Also, data flows from data stores might be outputs. For example, before Jack places an order with a supplier, he will need to view the supplier information. So he will need a list of suppliers with contact details and product information so that he can make an informed choice of which supplier to honour with an order for a truckload of mushy peas. The list of suppliers, and the order itself, are both outputs.

It may not be necessary to identify every possible output in advance. Most modern database packages include simple reporting tools and wizards so that most users will be able to set up their own queries as required.

When designing outputs, it is not wise to sit at a PC and start pressing buttons straight away. It is far better to start with a pencil and paper and draft a rough design for the screen or report.

Pre-formatted design sheets are often used featuring XXXXs to represent alphanumeric characters and 9999s to represent numeric information (see Table 6.3 below). In this way, fields or columns can be quickly positioned on the design. Report headings and sub-headings will appear at the top of the design and on every new page. At the end of the report, some kind of summary, such as totals and a grand total for numerical fields, will normally be appropriate.

Additional features will depend upon the nature of the report, but the date and page numbers will usually appear. Related information such as patient name, address and telephone number will appear together in a sensible order. The key thing is to make the report clear and legible. This may mean including some white space around columns or headings so that the report does not appear too cramped. Also, it is often worth supporting rows and rows of figures with a chart or two picking out the key items of information.

Whether the output is on-screen or in the form of a written report, it must be carefully designed to suit the user. This usually means the outputs must be relevant and clear as a minimum requirement. Internal reports, such as the work rota in the Medical Centre, will normally be just that – relevant and clear. However, reports to the GPC might be crafted more carefully, perhaps highlighting key information through charts, or grouping related information together.

Another example of an external report might be the report to the PMA, which will list all the prescriptions issued by the Medical Centre over a given period. A short extract from the report might look like Table 6.2.

Table 6.2 *PMA report – weak design.*

NHS number	Patient name	Prescription date	Prescription	Diagnosis	Doctor
4534552	Wilf Carp	23/11/02	Paracetamol	Broken leg	McLean
3455622	Oliver Plum	12/12/02	Paracetamol	Paracetamol overdose	Hammler
4667782	Jason Spink	14/12/02	Paracetamol	Collapsed lung	McLean
6733332	Irene Skidmore	14/12/02	Penicillin	Gout	Prodder
4667782	Jason Spink	15/12/02	Cod liver oil	Collapsed lung	McLean
4667782	Jason Spink	16/12/02	Iron lung	Respiratory failure	Prodder

However, this is not a particularly well-designed report. The information is not in any significant order (just by date of entry), and nothing is highlighted as being particularly significant. No report headings or dates are in evidence. A more useful report might group the report by prescription, as prescriptions are the focus, and order by date within the prescription. A better report design might look like the one in Table 6.3.

Table 6.3 *PMA report design.*

Medical Centre at the University of Life

PMA Report – {report date}

Prescription: {prescription}

NHS number	Patient name	Prescription date	Diagnosis	Doctor	Amount (g)
9999999	XXXXXXXXXXXX XXXXXXXXXXXX	dd/mm/yy	XXXXXXXX XXXXXXXX XXXXXXXX	{doctor}	999
				Total	9999

Page no.

This design might produce a report like Table 6.4.

This is a clear and simple design with no frills as it is for the sole use of a government agency and is not for public view.

An example from Swillbuckets: Jack will want to send details of forthcoming events to the media and to club members. This report needs to be clear and well-presented as it is for public view. An example of this kind of output is shown in Table 6.5.

Table 6.4 *PMA report – good design.*

Medical Centre at the University of Life

PMA Report – 4th Quarter 2002

Prescription: Paracetamol

NHS number	Patient name	Prescription date	Diagnosis	Doctor	Amount (g)
4534552	Wilf Carp	23/11/02	Broken leg	McLean	50
3455622	Oliver Plum	12/12/02	Paracetamol overdose	Hammler	20
4667782	Jason Spink	14/12/02	Collapsed lung	McLean	100
				Total	170

Prescription: Penicillin

NHS number	Patient name	Prescription date	Diagnosis	Doctor	Amount (g)
2344552	Holly Skidmore	14/12/02	Gout	Prodder	50
5656632	Archie Bloggs	18/12/02	Lumbago	Squeam	100
				Total	150

Prescription: Cod Liver Oil

NHS number	Patient name	Prescription date	Diagnosis	Doctor	Amount (g)
4667782	Jason Spink	15/12/02	Collapsed lung	McLean	300
				Total	300

Prescription: Iron Lung (Ventilator)

NHS number	Patient name	Prescription date	Diagnosis	Doctor	Amount (g)
4667782	Jason Spink	16/12/02	Respiratory failure	Prodder	

Page 1 of 5

Image considerations such as a logo and the overall impression created by the reports will be important here.

Other reports will simply be on-screen reports. Here, the user will view one record at a time (e.g. members at Swillbuckets). Such screens will need to be simple and attractive. Additionally, there will need to be facilities to allow the user to move to other screens e.g. a 'Back' button and a 'Forward' button. Many of the issues of screen design will be looked at in the Input Design section (6.4.3). One key factor in output design, though, is to involve the user. Users get very frustrated with designs which don't quite fit the bill, especially if they have to use them day in day out.

Table 6.5 *Events List report.*

Date	Event Name	Artiste	Entrance Fee
	Swillbuckets Club December Events List		
11/12/02	Man of Men Competition	Sharon Twain Entertains	£5.00
12/12/02	Dan on Spoons	Dan Pickles	£1.50
16/12/02	A Right Good Do	Little and Lard	£3.00
19/12/02	5-legged Pig Race	Rocky Rocket and the Rockettes	*free*
24/12/02	Christmas Eve Extravaganza	Tracey Beardmore is Shirley Bassey	£5.78

compiled by Jack Trout (Secretary) tel: 5554448

6.4.2 Simple steps in output design

1   Decide on the purpose of the report.
This will involve talking to the user.

2   Decide how the report will be used.
Will the report be for internal use, or external use? Will it be required regularly or just in exceptional cases?

3   List the information to be included in the report.
What fields from the database will be included? Will there be any charts or multimedia output? Only include information the user wants. Just because information is available does not mean that it should be in the report.

4   Decide whether the output will be on-screen, printed or both.

5   Design the report.
This can be done on a piece of paper or using a pre-formatted design sheet.

6   Produce a prototype report.
This should be discussed with users before the final design is specified.

6.4.3 Input design

This phase of the design process focuses on getting data into the system as quickly and effectively as possible. The first part of the process is to determine exactly what we are going to put into the system. This can be achieved by listing all the attributes for each entity on our entity model. In other words, all the bits of data, such as Patient Name, Patient Address and so on, will need to be input somehow. In addition we will need to look at the DFDs to see what data is flowing into the system from external bodies. All of that data may well have to go into our system. The student list required for the registration of patients at the Medical Centre is an example of this.

Once we know what data is going in, we need to decide how it's going to get into the system. There are various input devices we might use. There are some devices which will input data automatically, such as barcode scanners. If possible, these should be used, as they reduce the risk of errors being made. However, in many cases this is not appropriate. After all, patients might not be too happy about having bar codes imprinted on their foreheads. On the other hand, it should be possible to arrange for the student lists arriving from the University to be easily imported into the 'Patient' table. The Centre would have to insist that the lists arrive in digital format and then a little program could be written to allow the receptionists to import the file into the system.

So we will need to go through all the inputs and decide how we are going to perform the input, automating it where possible. Often, manual inputs will be required and this is where forms, or data entry screens, are used.

Data entry screens

There is one key thing to consider when designing these screens. We should try, at all times, to minimize the amount of data being input and the number of keystrokes required to do it. We can do this by using data already in the system to calculate or produce other data items where possible. Also, we can introduce codes and abbreviations to save typing in long strings of data. If there is a limited range of possible inputs, we can list them and allow the user to click on the one they want.

At the Medical Centre, most of the patients are students, so if we wanted to store occupation information, we could set up the system so that 'Student' would be automatically entered on the screen. The receptionist could change this on the occasions that it did not apply.

There are a number of Human–Computer Interface (HCI) considerations to bear in mind when designing these screens:

- Data entry screens often require the user to enter the data from a paper form directly into the form on the screen. If this is the case, the form on the screen should be consistent with the paper form, as far as possible. Ideally, it should be identical. At the very least, the fields on the screen should be in the same sequence as those on the form.

- Generally, the data should be input into the form moving from left to right and from top to bottom.

- Similar types of information should be grouped together – e.g. name, address, phone number.

- Use headings and labels to help the user identify the data.

- Use comments and instructions to tell the user what to do.

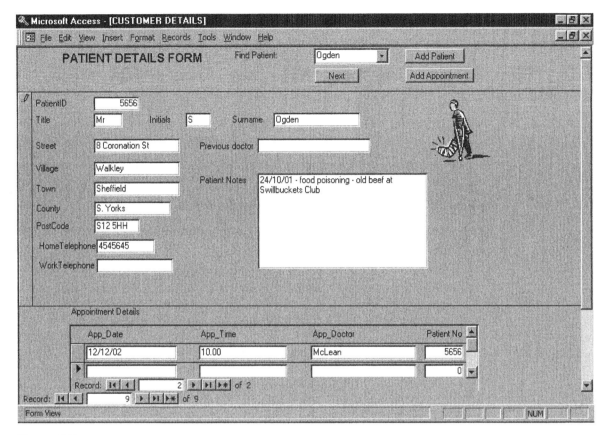

Figure 6.9
Well-designed data entry screen.

● Make it easy to move between screens – this may involve the use of sub-forms to minimize the need to move around (see Figure 6.9).

The example in Figure 6.9 shows a well designed data entry screen for the Medical Centre. The main form can be used for finding an existing patient or for entering a new patient's details. However, there is an appointment sub-form attached to it so that the receptionists can see previous appointments and add a new appointment without leaving the patient's main screen.

The screen looks clear and uncluttered. Note that the text is primarily lower case. This is easier to read than upper case. Also, the font needs to be easy to read, so avoid fancy fonts and italics. Use lines or boxes to separate different areas. The background should normally be plain. A simple colour scheme is fine, but avoid lots of different colours. Images and animations may get tedious by the time the user has input 200 new patients, so use with care.

Data validation

It is important to make every effort to ensure that the data entered into the system is accurate and sensible. This involves designing data validation checks. As mentioned above, the less data users need to enter, the fewer errors they can make. Additionally, we can check most of the data being entered to try to spot errors before they become part of the system.

These are the kinds of checks we can build in to data entry screens:

● Check that key and mandatory fields have data in them.

● Check that numeric data is within a sensible range – e.g. no-one can be aged 601 (indeed, very few reach 61 if registered at the Medical Centre).

● Check that data is of the right type e.g. a name with a '7' in it is unlikely to be accurate.

● Check that data is entered in the right order.

● Check that data is sensible; e.g. an appointment time of 3.30 a.m. might raise eyebrows.

All of these can be done automatically and any errors might generate a message like 'George, no-one was born on 15/h6/!%; have another try'. Generally, error messages should be simple and factual. Having just made yet another error, the data input clerk is normally in no mood for jokey messages.

6.4.4 Simple steps in input design

1 Identify the data to be input.

2 Determine the input method.

3 Design the screen.

4 Design the validation process.

6.4.5 User interface design

The user interface refers to the elements of a system through which users communicate with the system. Data input and output are a part of this, but there are other related elements. We are aiming to achieve a high-quality interface, by which we mean an interface that is easy to learn, easy to use and efficient. After a while, the interface should feel intuitive so that the user can move around the system without having to think.

Consistency is a key factor in making an interface easy to learn. The use of labels and icons must always be consistent. The same label or icon should always mean the same thing. Also, the way the screens are structured must be consistent and efficient.

For example, many systems use a menu structure to help users find the facility they want. The top-level menu will list all the main functions or operations performed by the system. There should be no more than six or seven of these. The user will choose one of these options and then be presented with a sub-menu. Very quickly, the user should reach the facility that he or she requires and will be able to run the program. Clearly, there will need to be user involvement in the design of the menus.

It is often a good idea to include a Help facility in the system. This might be an indexed user guide, or a link to a web site where help is available. Other user interface features to consider will be: check boxes; radio buttons; scroll bars; drop-down lists and so on. All of these can save users time and effort as well as make the interface attractive and easy to use. More of this in Chapter 8.

Summary

In this chapter, we have begun the process of specifying the requirements of the new system. Requirements specification continues in the next chapter, which involves the enhancement of the data model. This is more commonly referred to as normalization.

Exercises

6.1 Produce a decision table to model the logic in this scenario:
A postal delivery company delivers parcels air or rail transport. The price of delivery by air depends upon the weight of the parcel. There is a basic charge of £5 per kg up to 50 kg. Excess weight over 50 kg is charged at £3 per kilo.

Delivery by rail is charged at £3 per kg up to 50 kg and then £2 per kg. There is a special service guaranteeing same day delivery which carries an additional flat rate charge of £20.

Any deliveries overseas are charged at double the normal rate.

6.2 Produce a structured English specification for this scenario:
A travel agent has account customers and individual customers. Account customers who have spent over £25,000 in the past year get a discount of 25%. Otherwise, they get a 10% discount. Individual customers who have booked holidays previously get a 5% discount. New customers get no discount. Account customers who have spent over £10,000 in any previous year will receive offers of free tickets on selected routes.

6.3 Design a report for the Medical Centre showing the appointments for the following week. The report will be used by the receptionists to check patients as they arrive for their appointment, so consider what information will be required on the report.

CHAPTER 7

Normalization

7.1 | Normalization

Normalization is a bit like having a vaccine injected into your arm. It's painful (I've seen grown men cry), but it's better than the alternatives.

Normalization is a way of modelling the structure of the data. With a bit of luck, you should end up with the tables designed and ready to use.

You will already have done a version of this modelling of the data structure when you did your entity models. So why do it all again? Well, the entity models started from very general things, or entities, and then got more and more detailed. Normalization is the other way round. You start with all the bits of data lying around on forms or in filing cabinets and you sort them into groups of similar data. These end up being the tables, or data structure.

This is called 'bottom up' design. The aim is to help you understand better the data required by the new system, and to check that the entity model you have is accurate. Usually it's not, and you end up having to do another after normalization.

The other point is that entity modelling is a bit hit and miss, whereas normalization is based on mathematical principles and, if you do it right, should give you a bullet-proof design. It's the doing it right bit that can cause some pain.

7.1.1 What happens if data isn't normalized

We'll use Swillbuckets Country Club to demonstrate the nightmare that could happen if you don't normalize. As you may know, Swillbuckets prides itself on its meat dishes as well as the high-quality artistes who regularly entertain the members.

As a result of all these different activities, there are all sorts of data buzzing round the place. Here's a list of some of the data categories or fields; there would be more but these will do for now:

EventDate
ArtisteName
TelNo
cost
StartTime
DishName
IngredName
quantity
NoInStock

(The convention in this book is that where two words are required in the name, capital letters are used to denote this.)

We could just put all this data into one big table and start entering data. We would end up with something like Table 7.1.

Table 7.1 *Unnormalized data.*

Event Date	ArtisteName	TelNo	cost (£)	Start Time	DishName	IngredName	quantity	NoIn Stock
01/05/ 03	Tracey Beardmore is Shirley Bassey	33333	50	8.00	Chicken in a polystyrene tray	chicken	quarter	4320
						polystyrene	1	1044
02/05/ 03	Jade Green and her Dancing Chihuahuas	44444	80	7.00	Offal surprise and peas	sheep intestines	0.5 kg	202
						peas	28	550
04/05/ 03	Sharon Twain Entertains	55555	90	8.00	Skewered kidneys in lager	kidneys	6	4078
						lager	10	50
						skewer	1	45
07/05/ 03	Gypsy Ky-Lee Clairvoyant	66666	25	7.00	Crispy duck and crisps	duck	half	345
						prawn cocktail crisps	1	5500
08/05/ 03	Tracey Beardmore is Shirley Bassey	33333	50	7.30	Industrial strength chilli	old beef	1 kg	188
						tin of sauce	1	377
						rice	4 g	289
09/05/ 03	Jade Green and her Dancing Chihuahuas	44444	80	7.00	Offal surprise and peas	sheep intestines	0.5 kg	202
						peas	28	550

One or two problems are clear straight away. We are repeating all the information about an artiste every time we book them. For example, every time we book 'Jade Green and her Dancing Chihuahuas', we are also typing in the phone number and the cost. Since we already have this information, it is a waste of time and disk space to keep repeating it.

Another problem is the gaps that appear. The full effects of these gaps would not be seen until we tried to sort the information. If we sorted on ingredient (IngredName), say, to use as a shopping list, we'd end up with one looking like the one in Table 7.2.

Now I'm no TV chef, but I would suggest that 'Skewered kidneys in lager' would not normally have prawn cocktail crisps as a key ingredient. (Although, come to think of it, it might not be too bad....) Similarly, 'Industrial strength chilli' probably wouldn't benefit much from having polystyrene tipped in. You can see the sort of problems we're having here.

Table 7.2 *Sorted unnormalized data.*

Event Date	ArtisteName	TelNo	cost (£)	Start Time	DishName	IngredName	quantity	NoIn Stock
01/05/03	Tracey Beardmore is Shirley Bassey	33333	50	8.00	Chicken in a polystyrene tray	chicken	quarter	4320
						duck	half	345
07/05/03	Gypsy Ky-Lee Clairvoyant	66666	25	7.00	Crispy duck and crisps	lager	10	50
08/05/03	Tracey Beardmore is Shirley Bassey	33333	50	7.30	Industrial strength chilli	old beef	1 kg	188
						peas	28	550
						peas	28	550
						polystyrene	1	1044
06/05/03	Sharon Twain entertains	55555	90	8.00	Skewered kidneys in lager	potatoes	half a tin	5060
						prawn cocktail crisps	1	5500
						rice	4 g	289
						sheep intestines	0.5 kg	202
02/05/03	Jade Green and her Dancing Chihuahuas	44444	80	7.00	Offal surprise and peas	sheep intestines	0.5 kg	202
09/05/03	Jade Green and her Dancing Chihuahuas	44444	80	7.00	Offal surprise and Peas	skewer	1	45
						tin of sauce	1	377

Having gaps in the data structure has meant that we have lost our recipes, possibly forever. A sad loss for the culinary world.

Table 7.3 Unnormalized data with duplicate data.

Event Date	ArtisteName	TelNo	cost (£)	Start Time	DishName	IngredName	quantity	NoIn Stock
01/05/03	Tracey Beardmore is Shirley Bassey	33333	50	8.00	Chicken in a polystyrene tray	chicken	quarter	4320
01/05/03	Tracey Beardmore is Shirley Bassey	33333	50	8.00	Chicken in a polystyrene tray	polystyrene	1	1044
02/05/03	Jade Green and her Dancing Chihuahuas	44444	80	7.00	Offal surprise and peas	sheep intestines	0.5 kg	202
02/05/03	Jade Green and her Dancing Chihuahuas	44444	80	7.00	Offal surprise and peas	peas	28	550
04/05/03	Sharon Twain entertains	55555	90	8.00	Skewered kidneys in lager	kidneys	6	4078
04/05/03	Sharon Twain entertains	55555	90	8.00	Skewered kidneys in lager	lager	10	50
04/05/03	Sharon Twain entertains	55555	90	8.00	Skewered kidneys in lager	skewer	1	45
07/05/03	Gypsy Ky-Lee Clairvoyant	66666	25	7.00	Crispy duck and crisps	duck	half	345
07/05/03	Gypsy Ky-Lee Clairvoyant	66666	25	7.00	Crispy duck and crisps	prawn cocktail crisps	1	5500
08/05/03	Tracey Beardmore is Shirley Bassey	33333	50	7.30	Industrial strength chilli	old beef	1 kg	188
08/05/03	Tracey Beardmore is Shirley Bassey	33333	50	7.30	Industrial strength chilli	tin of sauce	1	377
08/05/03	Tracey Beardmore is Shirley Bassey	33333	50	7.30	Industrial strength chilli	rice	4 g	289
09/05/03	Jade Green and her Dancing Chihuahuas	44444	80	7.00	Offal surprise and peas	sheep intestines	0.5 kg	202
09/05/03	Jade Green and her Dancing Chihuahuas	44444	80	7.00	Offal surprise and peas	peas	28	550

Of course, we could just fill in the gaps with duplicate data: that would solve the sorting problem. That would give us a data model looking like Table 7.3.

However, there are still three types of problem with this data structure.

1   The insertion problem

Suppose we decide to buy some ingredients because they happen to be cheap and available. In fact, this happened only last week at Swillbuckets, when Seth Shepherd poached a few rabbits on the Chalfont estate. Jack Trout was quick to spot a commercial opportunity and a large black bag soon appeared at the Swillbuckets back door.

So now Jack has the new ingredient, rabbit, but where does he put it in our current design? He doesn't yet have a recipe to put it in or an event to serve it at. He can't just put it in the ingredients column, as that would mean leaving blanks in most of the other columns, and we know where that leads. If he sorted on ingredient, he would finish up with rabbit in the skewered kidneys. Not ideal.

2   The update problem

Let's think about sheep's intestines. On second thoughts, maybe not. Let's think about peas. Peas occurs twice in our list of ingredients. This is because Jade Green (and, indeed, her chihuahuas) is very partial to 'Offal surprise and peas'. As a result, every time she performs, she insists it's on the menu. So, in our current data structure, peas will be repeated every time Jade Green performs. Also, peas might occur in a number of different recipes and at different events.

At the moment, Jack has 28 tins of peas in stock. If he uses one up, he needs to update the data (change it to 27). But he doesn't just have to do this once, he has to go through all his data looking for every occurrence of peas and making the same update each time.

If he's fresh from a lunchtime session in Swillbuckets Bar, he's bound to miss some and then no one will know whether there are 27 or 28 tins in stock. Soon no one will believe the data. It'll have no integrity. A bit like Jack.

3   The deletion problem

Another problem reveals itself if we have to delete something. If somebody complains about the 'Industrial strength chilli' (and who can blame them?), or dies a painful death, Jack might have to take it off the menu. So he deletes the rows containing information about Industrial strength chilli. Unfortunately, he's also deleted the information about how much old beef he has in stock – 90 kg of the stuff to be exact. This is bad news because the Health Inspectors are not going to take kindly to finding 90 kg of old beef stuffed in the back of the fridge that Jack has forgotten about because he's deleted it from his database.

There are plenty of problems with the way this data is structured at the moment. So what's the solution? Splitting the data up into a number of smaller tables, instead of one big one. In other words – normalization. So let's do some before Swillbuckets gets shut down.

Normalization is quite difficult and complex. Sadly, it's also arguably the most important bit of SSADM. Life's cruel. If it wasn't so important, it would have been chucked in the bin years ago. Here are some simple tasks, but they aren't that simple. Don't panic if you don't get the hang of it first time. Almost nobody does. The trick is to keep hammering away at it until it gives in and reveals its secrets.

7.1.2 (Not so) simple tasks in normalization

1 Make sure you understand the data.
It's no good expecting to be able to breeze through normalization without first understanding the data. You must know what each bit of data is there for, what it relates to and how it's used. Hopefully, you've done this during the analysis phase.

2 Decide what to normalize.
The easiest way is to do it one form at a time, and then merge it all together. So that's what we'll do here. On the other hand, you could try to normalize all the data at once. This is not recommended if there are more than about 20 items of data in the system.

The Swillbuckets example above only shows nine fields of data, but in reality there would be many more: the address of the performers, their agents, the admission fee etc. So we'll tackle it one form at a time. I say 'form', but actually we want anything that's to be inputted into the system or outputted from it – things like invoices, lists of forthcoming events, recipes and stock lists. Also, we might need to add in new items that aren't currently in the system but will be in the new system we're designing. Figures 7.1–7.4 show a sample of the sort of thing we might normalize.

Figure 7.1
Forthcoming events list.

Swillbuckets Country Club

Forthcoming Events

4/12/02	8.00	Curry and peas night – eat, drink and be poorly	£1
7/12/02	7.30	Slide show with Eddie Jones – 'Stuffing dead voles'	
11/12/02	8.00	Fancy Dress Party – Theme: 'The Butcher's Shop'	£5
12/12/02	7.30	Dan Pickles on spoons plus buttered toast	£1
19/12/02	7.00	Annual 5-Legged Pig Race – Man and pig in harness!	
24/12/02	8.00	Christmas Eve Special 'A right good do' (volunteers please for balloon blowing and spittoon emptying) Admission by ticket only	£10
26/12/02	2.00	Boxing Day Tug o' war, fastest 6 pints, stomach throwing in the Swillbuckets Man of Men Competition	
27/12/02		Closed for refurbishment	

Events are free to members unless otherwise stated

Figure 7.2
Payslip.

Swillbuckets Payment Slip

Payment Date: 12/10/02

Deductions: £45 – damage to stage

Payee: Little and Lard

Payment method: Cash

Fee: £75.00

Net pay: £30

Figure 7.3
Membership form.

Swillbuckets Membership Form

Name: Wilf Trotter

Date: 20 November 2002

Address: Hag End Farm
Nether Bog
Muckthwaite
W. Yorks

Postcode: H34 2FT

Date of birth: 12 January 1904

Member Type: Free

Seconder: Josh Gitter

Interests: Brown water rafting
Coal sculpting
Reclaiming mine shafts

Level: Beginner
Expert
Expert

Do not write below this line or there will be trouble

For official use only

Member No: 5647

Fee: N/A

Figure 7.4
Event booking form.

Swillbuckets Event Booking Form

Date of event: 12/12/02

Name of event: Dan Pickles on Spoons

Artiste: Dan Pickles

Contact No: 2344556

Fee: £45

Status: Provisional/Confirmed

Special Requirements: 5 rounds of buttered toast
3 cups of tea
spare spoons

Signed: *Jack Trout*

Date: 14/11/02

That's enough to be going on with. We'll start with the Forthcoming Events List.

3 List all the fields on a normalization sheet.
You could use one like Table 7.4 (or just use some large, blank paper).

Table 7.4 *Forthcoming events list UNF.*

Normalization				
System: Swillbuckets				
Form/Report: Forthcoming Events List				
Author: Kevin Bowman				
Date: 20/6/03		**Page** 1 of 1		**Draft/**~~Final~~
Data Structure:				
UNF	**1NF**	**2NF**	**3NF**	**TABLE NAME**
EventDate				
StartTime				
EventName				
EntranceFee				
SpecialPoint				

All the fields of data from the Forthcoming Events List are listed in the column headed UNF – this stands for Unnormalized Form. The field called 'SpecialPoint' refers to any special information about an event. For example, volunteers are needed for the Christmas Eve Special to blow up balloons and empty spittoons. Let's hope they don't get confused and blow up the spittoon....

4 Find a key.
As mentioned in Chapter 3, a key is a way of identifying a form or a table, or whatever. Your key is your name, usually. It's how other people identify you. But it's not a brilliant key because there will be lots of people with the same name as you. A better key to identify you would be your National Insurance Number (or equivalent). It's unique. There are never two the same. That's why the government invented it. They could have used your name combined with your address as a way of identifying who you are. The problem is, people move house, whereas a National Insurance Number always stays the same.

Anyway, we need a key for the Forthcoming Events List.

Let's imagine there was a big pile of these lists and you had to find one particular one. What bit, or bits, of data would you need to know to find the list you wanted? Knowing one of the events wouldn't help – say 'Curry and peas night' – because that might appear on other lists. But if you knew one of the events and the date, that would do it. There would never be two

'Curry and peas nights' on the same day. That combination of event and date would never appear anywhere else.

So, we've established that the key will be 'Event name' and 'Event date' combined. (If you have a key made up of more than one bit of data, like this one, it's called a composite key.)

5   Underline the key bit(s) of data.
Just to show it's the key.

6   Find repeating groups.
The best way to do this is to draw a rough table showing the sort of data we're likely to get, like the one earlier (Table 7.1) which showed all the gaps before normalization. Use the fields as headings in the table. So you get something like Table 7.5.

Table 7.5 *Forthcoming Events List data.*

EventDate	EventName	Start Time	Entrance Fee	SpecialPoint
04/12/03	Curry and peas night	8.00	1.00	None
07/12/03	Slide show with Eddie Jones	7.30	0	None
11/12/03	Fancy dress party	8.00	5.00	Theme: Butcher's Shop
12/12/03	Dan Pickles on spoons	7.30	1.00	Buttered toast
19/12/03	5-legged pig race	7.00	0	None
24/12/03	Christmas Eve Special	8.00	10.00	Volunteers for balloon blowing
				Volunteers for spittoon emptying
				Ticket only

There are some gaps at the bottom of the table caused by the fact that there are three SpecialPoints for the Christmas Eve Special. We could fill in the gaps by duplicating all the Christmas Eve Special information:

24/12/03	Christmas Eve Special	8.00	10.00	Volunteers for balloon blowing
24/12/03	Christmas Eve Special	8.00	10.00	Volunteers for spittoon emptying
24/12/03	Christmas Eve Special	8.00	10.00	Ticket only

but we clearly have a repeating group here. Repeating groups are the ones with different values from the rest of the fields. In this case, it's the 'SpecialPoints' that are different. Everything else stays the same. You could say that for every event, there might be many 'SpecialPoints'. It's the 'many' bits that we call 'repeating groups'. So what do we do with them?

7 Split up the data structure.

Because we have repeating groups, we have to split up the data structure. We take away the repeating groups and make them into a separate group, or relation. We must take with this new group a copy of the key (Table 7.6). (The column headings will be explained as we go through the normalization process.)

Table 7.6 *Forthcoming Events List 1NF.*

Data structure:				
UNF	**1NF**	**2NF**	**3NF**	**TABLE NAME**
EventDate EventName StartTime ⟶ StartTime EntranceFee SpecialPoint	EventDate EventName StartTime EntranceFee EventDate EventName SpecialPoint			

8 Identify a key for the repeating group.

This new breakaway group currently has the same key as the unnormalized group. This is never right. In this case, you could not identify one particular 'SpecialPoint', by knowing the 'EventDate' and the 'EventName'. Let's say you knew the event was the Christmas Eve Special and the date was 24/12/01; you wouldn't be able to identify a particular 'SpecialPoint' as there are three possibilities – that's why we had to remove them. So you always need a different key for repeating groups. In this case, there's no option as there is only one bit of data not already in the key – 'SpecialPoint'. So we make this part of our composite key and now we can identify all data items. Our table is now in First Normal Form (1NF) and looks like Table 7.7.

Table 7.7 *Forthcoming Events List 1NF with key.*

Data structure:				
UNF	**1NF**	**2NF**	**3NF**	**TABLE NAME**
EventDate EventName StartTime ⟶ StartTime EntranceFee SpecialPoint	EventDate EventName StartTime EntranceFee EventDate EventName SpecialPoint			

The eagle-eyed among you will have noticed that the two new groups have fields in common, i.e. the original key. This will become important because these common fields will act as a link and allow a relationship between the groups when they become tables in a database.

9 Move to Second Normal Form.

Second Normal Form only applies to groups of data with composite keys – that's the good news. The bad news is that there will usually be at least one group with a composite key. In our case, both our groups have composite keys, so we need to examine both groups.

We are looking for non-key fields that are dependent upon only part of the composite key, not the whole thing. If we find any, we need to split them up. How do you know if a field is dependent upon another field or not?

This is the crunch question in normalization.

The best way to think about this is to ask the question: *What determines what?* For example, a worker's **pay_grade** determines his or her **pay**. If we know the **pay_grade**, we know the **pay**. So **pay** is dependent upon **pay_grade**.

The box with the arrow pointing at it is dependent upon the box with the arrow coming from it.

Here are some more examples: **doctor_no** determines **doctor_name** and **doctor_address**. If we know the doctor number, we know the doctor's name and address. So **doctor_name** and **doctor_address** are dependent upon **doctor_no**.

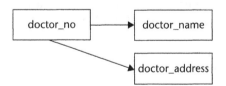

Car_registration_no determines **car_model**, **car_colour** and **engine_size**. If we know the registration number of a car, we will know the model, colour and engine size. So they are dependent upon **car_registration**.

It gets a little more complicated when a field is dependent upon a number of other fields. For example, in a university or college: **course_name**, **date** and **class_time** will determine **room_no**. You will have to know all three of the course name, the date and the time of the class, in order to know which room to go to. So **room_no** is dependent upon **course_name**, **date** and **class_time** combined.

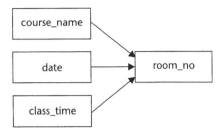

So let's have another look at our current table (7.7). Remember, we're interested in any non-key fields that might be dependent upon only a part of the composite key.

Let's look at the first group, the one with StartTime and EntranceFee as its non-key fields. We'll take one field at a time. For the field StartTime, do we need to know both EventDate and EventName in order to determine StartTime, bearing in mind there might be more than one event on a particular date? Well, we would certainly need to know the EventName in order to find out what time it started. But do we also need to know the date? Yes, because there might be many events with the same name (e.g. Dan Pickles on Spoons), but they might not have the same start times. We need to know which particular Dan Pickles on Spoons, i.e. the EventDate, in order to be sure of the start time. Knowing the EventDate by itself would be sufficient as long as there is never more than one event on a particular date. But let's assume there might be more than one. So, we need to know both fields in order to determine StartTime. This means it is dependent upon the whole key.

Now, EntranceFee; it's pretty much the same as StartTime. We would need to know both the EventDate and the EventName in order to be sure of the EntranceFee. So EntranceFee is dependent upon the whole key too.

So both our non-key fields are dependent upon the whole key. The data is now in Second Normal Form and our table looks like Table 7.8.

Table 7.8 *Forthcoming Events List 2NF (partly done).*

Data structure:				
UNF	1NF	2NF	3NF	TABLE NAME
EventDate EventName StartTime EntranceFee SpecialPoint	EventDate EventName StartTime EntranceFee EventDate EventName SpecialPoint	EventDate EventName StartTime EntranceFee		

That leaves us with the other group: EventDate, EventName and SpecialPoint. Well, they are all part of the key, so there are no non-key fields to worry about. Fantastic! Who said normalization was difficult? So, we just move them across into the Second Normal Form column (Table 7.9).

Table 7.9 *Forthcoming Events List 2NF.*

Data structure:				
UNF	1NF	2NF	3NF	TABLE NAME
EventDate EventName StartTime ──►EntranceFee SpecialPoint	EventDate EventName StartTime ──► EntranceFee	EventDate EventName StartTime ──► EntranceFee		
	EventDate EventName SpecialPoint	EventDate EventName ──► SpecialPoint		

10 Move to Third Normal Form.

This one applies to just non-key fields. We have to check to see if any non-key fields are dependent upon another non-key field rather than on the key. If there are any like this, we need to split them away to form a new group. We will choose a key for this new group and leave a copy of this key in the old group. This forms a link between the two groups.

Looking at our table, there is only one candidate. For a start, the second group (EventDate, EventName and SpecialPoint) contain no non-key fields, so we can forget about that group. The first group needs looking at, though, since there are two non-key fields in there (StartTime and EntranceFee). We need to be sure that one of them is not dependent upon the other. Well, is the EntranceFee determined by the start time? If we know the start time, do we always know the entrance fee? No. Is the start time determined by the entrance fee? No. They are both determined by the key: EventDate and EventName.

So there is no problem here, we can simply move both our groups over to the Third Normal Form column.

It is useful to give each group a name at this point, just so that we know which group we are talking about. These may end up being the table names in the final database. The final normalized table looks like Table 7.10.

Table 7.10 *Forthcoming Events List 3NF.*

Data structure:				
UNF	1NF	2NF	3NF	TABLE NAME
EventDate EventName StartTime ──►EntranceFee SpecialPoint	EventDate EventName StartTime ──► EntranceFee	EventDate EventName StartTime ──► EntranceFee	EventDate EventName StartTime ──► EntranceFee	EVENT
	EventDate EventName ──► SpecialPoint	EventDate EventName ──► SpecialPoint	EventDate EventName SpecialPoint	SPECIAL POINT

11 Celebrate vigorously.

However, before you get too carried away, remember that we've only done one form and there are a good few more to do.

The Swillbuckets Payment Slip, you may remember, looked like this:

Swillbuckets Payment Slip

Payment Date: 12/10/02   Deductions: £45 – damage to stage

Payee: Little and Lard   Payment method: Cash

Fee: £75.00   Net pay: £30

This is fairly easy to normalize, so we'll whiz through this one (Table 7.11).

Table 7.11 *Payment Slip UNF.*

Normalization				
System: Swillbuckets				
Form/Report: Payment Slip				
Author: Kevin Bowman				
Date: 20/6/03	**Page** 1 of 1		**Draft**/~~Final~~	
Data Structure:				
UNF	**1NF**	**2NF**	**3NF**	**TABLE NAME**
PaymentDate				
amount				
deductions				
payee				
PayMethod				

This table shows all the fields on the Payment Slip with the exception of the 'Net pay' field. This can be ignored for the time being as it can be calculated by subtracting the 'deductions' value from the 'amount' value. Any calculated fields do not normally need to be included in the normalization process.

Next we need to find a key. There's a bit of a problem here. Even if we had every field as part of a composite key, we couldn't be sure it would be unique. We might have more than one payment slip created on the same day, for the same artist (payee) for the same amount, with the same deduction etc. It's unlikely, but far from impossible.

In this situation, rather than have a huge key which is not necessarily unique, it's best to invent a field which is unique. The obvious choice is 'payment slip number'. This probably should have been on Jack's form anyway; he just didn't think of it. He doesn't like forms much and who can blame him?

So let's add 'PayslipNo' to our table and make it the key:

PayslipNo				
PaymentDate				
amount				
deductions				
payee				
PayMethod				

Simple Step 6 now requires us to identify repeating groups, so let's see what the data might look like in a table (Table 7.12).

Table 7.12 *Payment Slip data.*

PayslipNo	PaymentDate	amount	deductions	payee	PayMethod
1	12/10/01	75.00	45.00	Little and Lard	cash
2	15/12/01	90.00	0.00	Sharon Twain	cheque
3	8/11/01	50.00	0.00	Tracey Beardmore	cash
4	12/12/01	80.00	20.00	Jade Green	cash
5	12/12/01	25.00	0.00	Gypsy Ky-Lee	cash

There are no obvious problems of a repeating group nature. The only possibility would be if we wanted to allow for the possibility that there might be a number of deductions on a payslip. Deductions would then be a repeating group. However, Jack simply requires a total figure for deductions, not a detailed record.

Since there are no composite keys involved here, we can skip straight to Second Normal Form. So the Normalization table would currently look like Table 7.13.

Table 7.13 *Payment Slip 2NF.*

Data Structure:				
UNF	1NF	2NF	3NF	TABLE NAME
PayslipNo	PayslipNo	PayslipNo		
PaymentDate	PaymentDate	PaymentDate		
amount	amount	amount		
deductions	deductions	deductions		
payee	payee	payee		
PayMethod	PayMethod	PayMethod		

Now we're ready for Simple Step 10 – Move to Third Normal Form. This is where we consider the non-key fields to see if they are dependent upon other non-key fields rather than the key. If we find any that are dependent upon other non-key fields, we will remove them into a separate group.

We need to look at each non-key field in turn. Let's start with PaymentDate. Does this field depend upon any of the other non-key fields? Does it depend upon amount? If we knew the amount, would we always know the payment date? No. If we knew the payee, would we always know the payment date? No. We would need to know the specific payslip (PayslipNo), in order to know the payment date.

If we go through each field in turn, we find that they all depend on the key, PayslipNo, with one possible exception. Let's just think about PayMethod. It's possible that each payee might have a particular method for being paid. So Gypsy Ky-Lee might only accept cash, for example. So, it could be argued that PayMethod depends upon payee.

If we decided that this was the case, we would take payee and PayMethod and put them in a separate group, with payee as the key. A copy of the key (payee) is left in the other group to act as a link, or foreign key. So the Third Normal Form table would look like Table 7.14.

Table 7.14 *Payment Slip 3NF – provisional.*

Data Structure:				
UNF	1NF	2NF	3NF	TABLE NAME
PayslipNo PaymentDate amount deductions payee PayMethod	PayslipNo PaymentDate amount deductions payee PayMethod	PayslipNo PaymentDate amount deductions payee PayMethod	PayslipNo PaymentDate amount deductions payee* payee PayMethod	

The little asterisk next to 'payee' in the top group shows that this is the link field, or foreign key, as it is known.

Having done that, Jack Trout then informs us that some artistes, such as Sharon Twain, aren't bothered whether they get paid by cash, cheque or free sherry, as long as they get paid. So, we would need to know the 'PayslipNo' after all in order to determine whether it was cash or cheque, or free sherry at the bar. So 'PayMethod' is not dependent upon 'payee' in all cases, it's dependent upon the key after all.

So we need to hastily redraw our table and simply move the group across from Second Normal Form to Third Normal Form (Table 7.15).

We'll call this table 'PAYMENT', and that's another form done.

Table 7.15 *Payment Slip 3NF – final version.*

Data Structure:				
UNF	1NF	2NF	3NF	TABLE NAME
<u>PayslipNo</u> PaymentDate amount ———▶ deductions payee PayMethod	<u>PayslipNo</u> PaymentDate amount ———▶ deductions payee PayMethod	<u>PayslipNo</u> PaymentDate amount ———▶ deductions payee PayMethod	<u>PayslipNo</u> PaymentDate amount deductions payee PayMethod	PAYMENT

Now it's time to consider the membership form. Just to remind you, here's what it looks like (Figure 7.5).

Figure 7.5
Membership form.

Swillbuckets Membership Form

Name:	Wilf Trotter	**Date:**	20 November 2002
Address:	Hag End Farm Nether Bog Muckthwaite W. Yorks		
Postcode:	H34 2FT	**Date of birth:**	12 January 1904
Member Type:	Free	**Seconder:**	Josh Gitter
Interests:	Brown water rafting Coal sculpting Reclaiming mine shafts	**Level:**	Beginner Expert Expert

Do not write below this line or there will be trouble

For official use only

Member No: 5647   **Fee:** N/A

This form is filled in when a new member joins Swillbuckets. It's a little more complex than the last, so we'll take it step by step. Let's list all the fields in the usual way (Table 7.16).

The next simple step requires us to identify a key field. We're in luck here, as Jack Trout has had the wisdom and foresight to include 'Membership No' on his form. It's called 'MemberNo' in our list of fields. Each member will have a different number allocated to them, so each one is unique. This makes it an ideal candidate for our key field. So without further ado, let's underline it (Table 7.17).

Now we're looking for repeating groups. Let's draw our table with some sample data (Table 7.18).

Table 7.16 *Membership form UNF.*

Normalization				
System: Swillbuckets				
Form/Report: Membership form				
Author: Kevin Bowman				
Date: 20/6/03	**Page** 1 of 1		**Draft/~~Final~~**	
Data Structure:				
UNF	**1NF**	**2NF**	**3NF**	**TABLE NAME**
date				
name				
address				
PostCode				
DateOfBirth				
type				
seconder				
interest				
level				
MemberNo				
RegFee				

Table 7.17 *Membership Form with key.*

Data Structure:				
UNF	**1NF**	**2NF**	**3NF**	**TABLE NAME**
<u>MemberNo</u> date name address PostCode DateOfBirth type seconder interest level RegFee				

You can see the problem here. We have repeating groups caused by the 'interest' and 'level' fields. There are multiple values of these for each 'MemberNo' (the key). So we remove them into another group taking a copy of the key with us. Table 7.19 shows the data in Second Normal Form.

Table 7.18 *Membership data.*

Member No	date	name	address	PostCode	DateOf Birth	type	seconder	interest	level	RegFee
5647	20/11/99	Wilf Trott	Hag End Farm	H34 2FT	12/1/04	F	Josh Gitter	brown water rafting	B	n/a
								coal sculpting	E	
								mine shaft reclaiming	E	
1234	12/3/94	Harry Babb	12 Park St	H1 3GH	14/2/11	R	Ewan Spratt	street cleaning	E	£10
								industrial sewing	B	
								cheese shaping	C	

Table 7.19 *Membership form 1NF.*

Data Structure:				
UNF	1NF	2NF	3NF	TABLE NAME
MemberNo date name ———→ address PostCode DateOfBirth type seconder interest level ⌐ RegFee	MemberNo date name address PostCode DateOfBirth type seconder RegFee MemberNo interest level			

The next simple step is to identify a key for this new group. In this case, we can identify a specific interest of a member if we know the member number and the interest. We don't need to know the level as well. So the composite key would be: 'MemberNo' and 'interest' (Table 7.20).

You will doubtless have remembered that moving to Second Normal Form requires us to examine only groups of data with composite keys. We need to check if the non-key field, 'level', is dependent upon both of the key fields in our second group. Do we have to know both the member number and the interest in order to identify the level? Yes we do. So, level is dependent upon both our key fields. We can move swiftly on through Second Normal Form (Table 7.21).

The move to Third Normal Form requires us to look at the other group. Here we are checking that non-key fields are not dependent upon other non-key fields, but are dependent upon the key only.

Table 7.20 *Membership form 1NF with keys.*

Data Structure:				
UNF	1NF	2NF	3NF	TABLE NAME
MemberNo date name address PostCode DateOfBirth type seconder interest level RegFee	MemberNo date name address PostCode DateOfBirth type seconder RegFee MemberNo interest level			

Table 7.21 *Membership form 2NF.*

Data Structure:				
UNF	1NF	2NF	3NF	TABLE NAME
MemberNo date name address PostCode DateOfBirth type seconder interest level RegFee	MemberNo date name address PostCode DateOfBirth type seconder RegFee MemberNo interest level	MemberNo date name address PostCode DateOfBirth type seconder RegFee MemberNo interest level		

The one possible candidate here is the 'RegFee' field. We need to know how that is determined. Jack tells us that there are three possible fees. Membership is free if the person is a pensioner when they join Swillbuckets. This is denoted by an 'F' for free in the 'Type' field. Membership is £10 if the person is unemployed when they join. This is denoted by 'R' for reduced in the 'type' field. Finally, membership is standard for everyone else. The standard fee is £25.

This tells us that the 'RegFee' field is dependent upon the 'type' field. If we know the type of membership – free, reduced or standard – we know the fee. So we need to take the 'type' and 'RegFee' fields out of the group, leaving a copy of the determinant field, 'type', behind. If we add the table names, our form is now normalized (Table 7.22).

Table 7.22 *Membership form normalized.*

Data Structure:				
UNF	**1NF**	**2NF**	**3NF**	**TABLE NAME**
MemberNo	MemberNo	MemberNo	MemberNo	
date	date	date	date	
name	name	name	name	MEMBER
address	address	address	address	
PostCode	PostCode	PostCode	PostCode	
DateOfBirth	DateOfBirth	DateOfBirth	DateOfBirth	
type	type	type	type	
seconder	seconder	seconder	seconder	
interest	RegFee	RegFee		
level			type	MEMBER
RegFee	MemberNo	MemberNo	RegFee	TYPE
	interest	interest		
	level	level	MemberNo	MEMBER
			interest	INTEREST
			level	

The final form we're going to consider from Swillbuckets is the Event Booking Form. Jack Trout uses this form to store information about how a booking is progressing. As soon as it's confirmed in writing by the artiste, Jack draws a ring round 'Confirmed' and moves it into a different shoebox. Figure 7.6 shows a copy of the form.

Figure 7.6
Event booking form.

Swillbuckets Event Booking Form

Date of event: 12/12/02
Name of event: Dan Pickles on Spoons
Artiste: Dan Pickles   **Contact No:** 2344556
Fee: £45   **Status:**   Provisional/Confirmed
Special Requirements: 5 rounds of buttered toast
                          3 cups of tea
                          spare spoons

Signed: *Jack Trout*   **Date:** 14/11/02

Some of the information on this form is recorded elsewhere. You may remember that EventName and EventDate are two of the fields in the first form we looked at, the Forthcoming Events List, so we need to be careful we're not recording the same information twice. Fortunately, SSADM takes care of this for us. Let's start filling in our normalization form in the usual way (Table 7.23).

Table 7.23 *Event booking form UNF.*

Normalization				
System: Swillets				
Form/Report: Event Booking form				
Author: Kevin Bowman				
Date: 20/9/03		**Page** 1 of 1		**Draft/~~Final~~**
Data Structure:				
UNF	**1NF**	**2NF**	**3NF**	**TABLE NAME**
EventDate				
EventName				
artiste				
ContactNo				
fee				
status				
SpecReq				
BookDate				

The key looks like being a combination of EventName and EventDate just as it was in the Forthcoming Events List. (Remember that we can't just have EventDate, as Jack might want to put on more than one event on a particular day). However, this only works if there is only ever one artiste at an event. We need to clarify this with Jack.

Jack informs us that at the moment he only has one artiste per event. This is due to an unfortunate incident a few years ago. He booked Jade Green and her Dancing Chihuahuas on the same bill as Leapy Len's Flea Circus. Apparently, the chihuahuas were soon dancing in a more frenzied fashion than usual and the fleas were never seen again.

Having said that, Jack would still like the option of having more than one act per event, so we have to allow for this possibility. This means that 'artiste' needs to be part of the composite key. Let's have a look at the sort of data we might get in tabular format (Table 7.24).

We can see that the special requirement field (SpecReq) is causing a problem by forcing us to repeat the data for the other fields or leave blanks. We need to remove this field along with a copy of the key in order to move to First Normal Form (Table 7.25).

The key for this new group will be the key for the unnormalized data plus SpecReq (Table 7.26).

Excellent. Now let's move to Second Normal Form. We check to see if the non-key fields are dependent upon the whole of the key. There is one field that needs attention, the ContactNo field. It's got nothing to do with EventDate or EventName but everything to do with artiste. ContactNo is

Table 7.24 *Event booking data.*

EventDate	EventName	artiste	ContactNo	fee	status	SpecReq	BookDate
12/11/02	Slide show with Eddie Jones	Eddie Jones	2242343	£50	C	projector	24/10/02
12/12/02	Dan Pickles on spoons	Dan Pickles	2344556	£45	C	5 rounds of buttered toast	14/11/02
						3 cups of tea	
						spare spoons	
24/12/02	Christmas Party	Bobby Crash	2343454	£85	P		10/11/02
31/12/02	New Year Do	Sharon Twain	2657378	£75	C	extra sherry	23/10/02
						room for the night	
						ambulance on standby	

Table 7.25 *Event booking data 1NF.*

Data Structure:				
UNF	**1NF**	**2NF**	**3NF**	**TABLE NAME**
EventDate EventName artiste ──────▶ ContactNo fee status SpecReq BookDate	EventDate EventName artiste ContactNo fee status BookDate EventDate EventName artiste SpecReq			

Table 7.26 *Event booking form 1NF with key.*

Data Structure:				
UNF	**1NF**	**2NF**	**3NF**	**TABLE NAME**
EventDate EventName artiste ──────▶ ContactNo fee status SpecReq BookDate	EventDate EventName artiste ContactNo fee status BookDate EventDate EventName artiste SpecReq			

determined by artiste alone. So we need to place artiste and ContactNo into a separate group leaving a copy of the determinant field, artiste behind (Table 7.27).

Table 7.27 *Event booking form 2NF.*

Data Structure:				
UNF	1NF	2NF	3NF	TABLE NAME
EventDate EventName artiste ContactNo fee status SpecReq BookDate	EventDate EventName artiste ContactNo fee status BookDate EventDate EventName artiste SpecReq	EventDate EventName artiste fee status BookDate artiste ContactNo EventDate EventName artiste SpecReq		

All the other non-key fields are dependent upon the whole of the key, so we don't need any more changes for Second Normal Form.

Third Normal Form requires us to check that there are no non-key fields dependent upon other non-key fields. So let's have a look. The bottom two groups aren't affected because there is only one non-key field in each group.

In the top group, fee, status and BookDate are all dependent upon the key not each other, so there's no problem here. Straight into Third Normal Form (Table 7.28) and we've almost finished normalizing our four forms. We'll give the groups of data names and move on to the final task of normalization.

7.2 ▌ Rationalization

This final task is called rationalization and is very easy. We've been gathering data from various forms, and in the real world there would be many more than the four we've looked at here. So we would end up with a large number of normalized groups. Rationalization attempts to merge some of these together, so we haven't got quite so many.

The idea is that if any of our groups have the same keys, then really they should be in the same group. So we need to see our groups and their keys. Below are the data groups, or relations, obtained from each form.

Table 7.28 *Event booking form normalized.*

Data Structure:				
UNF	**1NF**	**2NF**	**3NF**	**TABLE NAME**
EventDate EventName artiste ——▶ ContactNo fee status SpecReq BookDate	EventDate EventName artiste ——▶ ContactNo fee status BookDate	EventDate EventName artiste ——▶ fee status BookDate	EventDate EventName artiste fee status BookDate	BOOKING
	EventDate EventName artiste ——▶ SpecReq	artiste ——▶ ContactNo	artiste ContactNo	ARTISTE
		EventDate ——▶ EventName artiste SpecReq	EventDate EventName artiste SpecReq	ARTISTE REQ

Forthcoming Events List

EVENT	SPECIALPOINT
EventDate	*EventDate
EventName	*EventName
StartTime	SpecialPoint
EntranceFee	

Payment Slip

PAYMENT
PayslipNo
PaymentDate
amount
deduction
*payee
PayMethod

Membership Form

MEMBER	MEMBER TYPE	MEMBER INTEREST
MemberNo	type	*MemberNo
date	RegFee	interest
name		level
address		
PostCode		
DateOfBirth		
*type		
seconder		

Event Booking Form

BOOKING	ARTISTE	ARTISTE REQS
*EventDate	artiste	EventDate
*EventName	ContactNo	EventName
*artiste		*artiste
fee		SpecReq
status		
BookDate		

You might be tempted to think that because EventName appears in a number of keys, these groups can be merged. However, the whole key has to be identical for merging to take place.

It appears that there are no tables which share the same key, so no merging can take place. If we had normalized every form at Swillbuckets, however, it is likely there would have been some rationalization required.

Once rationalization is complete, we are in a position to compare the Required Logical Entity Model, completed in the last chapter (Figure 6.4) with the relations produced by normalization. Any enhancements required will now need to be built into the final entity model.

Just from the forms looked at above, there are a number of enhancements identified by normalization. Instead of simply having a MEMBER table, with all the data concerning members thrown in, we now see the need to have three tables: MEMBER, MEMBER TYPE and MEMBER INTEREST.

Similarly, there is a need to hold information about the requirements of artistes which we have called ARTISTE REQ and their payment which has resulted in the PAYMENT table. Also, the SPECIAL POINT entity has been added to store any special points about a particular event.

The process of rationalization would require us to merge together the FOOD ORDER and DRINK ORDER tables as, logically, they both have the same key – Order No.

Bearing these enhancements in mind, we can rebuild the Swillbuckets entity model.

7.3 | Rebuild the entity model

The model must be remodelled once again, to take into account the changes identified by normalization (Figure 7.7).

A number of issues regarding attributes have been resolved. For example, the key for EVENT has been finalized as EventNo as in the normalized tables, not a composite key of EventName and EventDate. We could have kept these two attributes as the primary key, but it is easier to use EventNo. In this situation where there is more than one possible primary key, the keys concerned are called candidate keys. As long as we remember to use EventNo as the primary key at all times, there will be no problem.

Figure 7.7
Swillbuckets entity
model after
normalization.

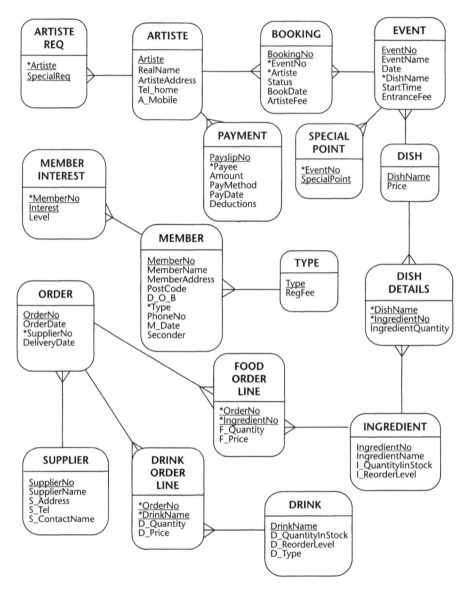

One or two synonyms have been identified. These are attributes with different names, but which are logically the same. For example, Payee in PAYMENT is the same as Artiste, which is fortunate as Payee is our link or foreign key. We could change Payee to Artiste or, if it's clearer, we can keep it as Payee.

7.4 Entity/function matrix

So far we have modelled the processes or functions using DFDs and the data structure using entity models for the required system. A third (and final) view of the new system is required to consider how the system will be affected by time. Our DFDs tell us what events or functions are likely to occur. Our entity model tells us what the data looks like. We now need to check that all the events can be accommodated by our data model. It may be that we have missed some events, or functions, from our DFDs, in which case we will need to update them. Or we may have missed a data item needed by a function. The entity function matrix allows us to check this.

The matrix pulls together the two previous views of the system and allows us to check that each entity has a beginning and an end, i.e. a function which creates it and a function which deletes it or archives it. The ability to delete an entity is particularly important; otherwise entities will carry on expanding forever. Similarly, we should check that each entity is used once it's in the system. After all, there's no point in collecting information about, say, drugs, if there isn't a means in the system to use the information. We don't want it just sitting around doing nothing. We have receptionists for that.

So we need to check if each entity is born, has a full and purposeful life, and then dies.

Creating an entity/function matrix is simple. Here are the steps.

7.4.1 Simple steps in creating an entity/function matrix

1 List the entities and functions.
Create the matrix on a piece of paper by listing all the entities down the side and all the functions across the top. You may need a large piece of paper to do this.

2 Create a grid.
Draw lines to divide the paper up into cells.

3 Fill in the grid.
This is done by looking at the DFDs and entering one of these possible options: **I** (Insert), **R** (Read), **M** (Modify), **D** (Delete) or **A** (Archive). Cells in the grid can be left blank if the function has no effect on the entity.

4 Check that each row (entity) has a full life.
In other words, it should be have an **I**, at least one **R** or **M** and a **D** or an **A**. Often there are no functions in the DFDs to create an entity or to delete the entity. These functions will need to be added to the DFDs. Occasionally, an entity will have more than one **I**. This needs looking at, as it implies that the entity is created more than once by different functions. There may be inconsistencies here.

5 Update the DFDs
There will normally be some changes required to the DFDs as a result of this process.

Table 7.29 is a section from an entity function matrix for the Medical Centre (not all functions and entities are shown).

In the Medical Centre, we can see that nothing is ever deleted apart from when an appointment is cancelled. We would need to discuss with Betty

Table 7.29 *Entity/function matrix – Medical Centre.*

Entity	1.1 Register Patient	1.2. Allocate patient to doctor	1.3 Inform GPC	2.1.Create appointment	2.2 Amend appointment	2.3 Cancel appointment	3.1 Receive patient for appointment	3.2 Diagnose illness or refer	3.3 Prescribe treatment	3.4 Create repeat prescription	3.5 Receive and check discount
Doctor											
Appointment				I	R/M	D	R/M				
Patient	I	M	R					R/M	R		
Prescription									I	M	R/M
Referral								I			
Drug									R		

and George a strategy for deleting records. Obviously we would want to keep patient records until the patient dies or leaves the Centre. We may be required to archive them for a period of time after death in case there are any queries about treatment. Perish the thought. These functions will need to be added to the required DFDs so that they appear in the final system.

It might also be noted that the Doctor entity is never inserted. This may not be viewed as a problem since it will happen only rarely, but the new system must allow us to perform this function.

Summary

We have focused very much on normalization in this chapter. This is because it is a crucial part of systems analysis and is relatively difficult to learn. This completes the specification of requirements and it now becomes a simple matter of sorting out a few physical design issues before we can start implementing the new system. The next chapter looks at the technical and physical design techniques required.

Exercises

7.1 Normalize the following data taken from a student assessment form, bearing in mind that students will take a number of modules:

Student Number
Student Name
Student Address

Module Code
Module Name
Module Mark
Module Grade

7.2 Normalize this form:

Purchase Order (Customer copy) Order: 345

To:

     Jack Trout
     Swillbuckets Club
     West Yorkshire

8/12/2002

From:

     Cooper's Brewery
     15 Brewery St
     Fillem

Product No	Name	Quantity	Price
10	Babycham	400	1.50
25	Old Firtle	25	30.00
48	Egg nog	20	2.50
28	Red Nose bitter	30	25.00

Total cost: 3536.00

CHAPTER 8

Technical and Physical Design

8.1 | Technical design and physical design

The technical design involves making any final decisions concerning the technical environment. We have already decided on the broad components of our system in both case studies. However, we now need to consider details like the exact specification of the PCs we will need. Which vendor should we choose to buy from? Can the required software be bought off the shelf? Or will it need developing? We will certainly need to discuss these issues with suppliers of equipment before reaching any decisions.

In a large system, it may be necessary to compile a list of options, much as we did for the Business Systems Options in Chapter 5. The same process of identifying the options, analysing costs and benefits and choosing the best option would apply.

Some organizations have detailed information systems policies that might well include service level agreements. Service level agreements specify the level of service that users can expect from the information systems. In this kind of environment, we need to be sure that our technical environment can meet the demands of the agreements.

The main aim of physical design is to design the physical system such that the performance is acceptable to the user and data integrity and security are guaranteed. In order to create the design, the analyst will need:

- the normalized tables
- attribute details
- interface requirements
- data volume estimates
- service level requirements
- security needs

We already have much of this information but have not, so far, considered the need to ensure that we have sufficient storage capacity in our system to store all the data. In order to be sure of this, we will have to calculate roughly how much storage space our system will require in the foreseeable future. This technique is called volumetrics and will be described shortly.

The main areas to be considered in physical design are:

- the performance of the system

- the user friendliness of the system

- response times

- security aspects

- accessibility

- the flexibility of the system – it's ability to develop as required

It is not difficult to imagine the impact on the user if any one of these areas is not functioning properly.

Very often it is impossible to make an informed choice of technical options until we have considered the physical design of our proposed system. These two activities must, to some extent, run in parallel rather than occur sequentially.

8.1.1 Design detailed user interface

A more detailed look at the user interface is now required. We have already specified some general principles in Chapter 6, but there are still some important decisions to make. As mentioned earlier, the key to a successful interface design is consistency. A set of rules or standards for the interface must be decided upon and used throughout. This makes the system easy to learn and gives it an intuitive feel. If, for example, the 'Print' button is situated in the bottom left-hand corner in one screen, it must be situated there in all the others, so that the users instinctively know where it is. A number of industry standards for interface design already exist and it seems sensible to adopt one of these.

While colour schemes should be consistent too, there may be some room for flexibility here. The user may wish to have different colours to denote different parts of the system. For example, Jack Trout might find it helpful to have a background of insipid puce for all the artiste screens and one of bile green for the food-related screens. This might add to the intuitive nature of the system. However, whatever colour scheme is used, the first priority is to make sure the text is clear and readable. That usually means dark text on a light background.

Readability is not improved by flashing purple labels on a black background.

On the subject of text, the choice of fonts is important. Lower-case serif fonts are the easiest to read. Examples of serif fonts are Times Roman and

Garamond. They have little hooks on the letters which allow the user's eye to skim across them quickly and easily. Avoid using italics and obscure or childish fonts.

The layout of the screens needs careful thought. There is a balance to be achieved between having all the necessary information available to the user on one screen and making the screen too cluttered. Screens should not be overloaded with navigation buttons and sub-forms. It may be necessary to create an additional screen if one screen is overloaded.

A good idea is to have an 'Escape to Main Menu' button on each key screen so that if users get confused, they have a route back to the safe haven which is the opening screen. Try to make this opening screen, the main menu, as welcoming as possible. This might be done with a welcome message, a logo or banner and use of colour.

8.1.2 Prototyping

Prototyping has developed as a response to some of the problems identified with SSADM and similar structured systems analysis methodologies. These problems are:

- implementation is delayed
- users are resistant
- the process takes too long
- diagrams are misunderstood

Prototyping attempts to solve these problems by the building of a cut-down version of the system as part of the design process. This allows the user to evaluate one or more prototypes and become more involved in the process. This also saves time by avoiding the need for lots of diagrams.

It is often a good idea to prototype one or two different user interfaces at this point in order to involve the user and to establish some clear preferences. The design of the user interface will have implications for the choice of technical environment. For example, one of our prototype interfaces might require a colour monitor to be effective. However, we might have decided on black and white monitors as a technical systems option. Should the preferred interface design drive the choice of hardware or should the choice of hardware drive the interface design? We will have to make this kind of awkward decision at this stage.

Prototypes can be generated very quickly using various high-level tools such as application generators. Since little time needs investing in them, they can be scrapped or radically altered if necessary without significant costs. They allow the user to visualize a range of options, to use them and to evaluate them. Usually a hybrid design is the preferred option after evaluation.

The analyst must be careful not to raise expectations unrealistically, however. Having seen the analyst generate a prototype interface in a couple of hours, the user may well expect the final system to be delivered in a couple of days. If so, the user is likely to be grossly disappointed, as there is still considerable work to do. That aside, prototyping is usually a very worthwhile technique providing high-quality feedback for the analyst.

8.1.3 Simple steps in prototyping

1   Discuss the options for screen designs with users.
We will need to be aware of any constraints and make the user aware of the scope of prototyping.

2   Build a prototype – quickly.
The prototype will need to take into account the chosen Business System Option, the entity model and the DFDs.

3   Demonstrate the prototype.
It will be necessary to set up this session carefully. The prototype must be installed on the user's workstation in advance and tested with sample data.

4   Evaluate the prototype.
This must be done in consultation with the user. The prototype may go straight in the bin, or there may be elements in it that the user likes. Either way, the analyst will have learnt something.

5   Build another prototype.
Hopefully, this is the end of the prototyping stage, but be prepared for another trip round the loop.

8.1.4 Interface flow diagrams

The ability to navigate easily between screens is another key aim of interface design. Ideally, the design should follow the likely flow of work as the user uses the system. This will give the user confidence in the system and increase efficiency. This aim can be achieved by the use of interface flow diagrams and by consideration of the required entity model, to identify key relationships. These diagrams in combination with prototyping provide an effective tool for the analyst.

The diagrams model the possible movement between screens available to the user. They provide an overview of the structure of the interface. Figure 8.1 is an example of one for part of the Medical Centre.

This shows the appointments sub-system and some related areas. Since APPOINTMENT has relationships with PATIENT and DOCTOR on the entity model, we would expect to see a similar set of relationships in the interface design. Clearly, there are a number of other ways in which the navigation around the system could be arranged; hence the need for prototype interfaces to aid selection.

Figure 8.1
Interface design
diagram.

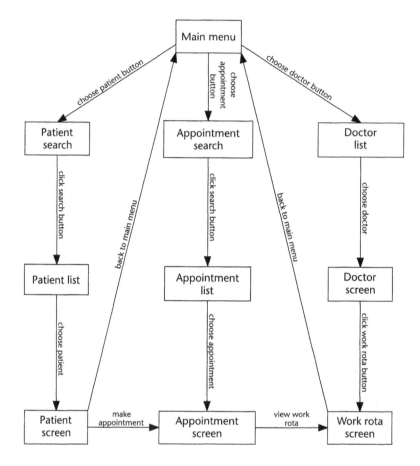

8.2 | Database design

Most systems will require the creation of a relational database – certainly our case study systems will. A relational database is defined by Connolly and Begg (1999) as 'a collection of normalized relations'. We will have spent considerable time and energy in designing these 'normalized relations' for our new system. Techniques such as normalization may have left us feeling weak and confused. However, it's all been worth it, because we can now start implementing our database.

Before we set up the tables in our Database Management System (such as Access or Oracle), we need to plan the detailed field formats. Broadly speaking, we will need to do the following:

● Each table (or relation) identified through entity modelling and normalization (i.e. on our required entity model) will become a table in our database.

● Each attribute on our required entity model will become a field in our database.

- Primary keys and foreign keys on our entity model will be translated onto our database structure, checking that foreign keys are at the 'many' end of the relationships.

- Each attribute will require a name, a field length, a data type (usually Text or Number) and possibly an input mask and validation rules (see below). Data integrity must be promoted through validation rules built into the format of the field.

The promotion of data integrity can take a number of forms. We can, for example, limit the range of possible inputs into a field. The Medical Centre could set the range of permissible inputs into 'Patient Age' to 0–120. In the case of Dr McLean's patients, that could be 0–65 without much danger of causing problems. Input masks ensure that data is entered in a specified format. This is particularly important in fields such as 'Postcode'.

Some DBMS allow the use of combo boxes in the design of the interface. These allow the user to choose from a list of prescribed choices. The chosen option is then entered into the field automatically so there is no possibility of error. This can only be used when there are only a limited number of possible entries, such as 'Doctor Name'.

8.2.1 Indexes

We will also need to design the indexes for our database. Particular fields, or combinations of fields, can be indexed. This means that an index file is kept, by the DBMS, recording the location of specific records and the order in which they need to be presented. These records can then be quickly located and presented in the particular order specified. For example, we could set up an index to list patients alphabetically by their surnames. This would allow the DBMS to locate and order the records much more quickly than if no such index existed.

We must consider very carefully, in consultation with the user, exactly what indexes need to be set up. Most modern DBMS systems will automatically produce an index for each table based on the primary key of the table. Additional indexes will depend upon what queries the user anticipates having to deal with regularly and what reports we have already identified in the system requirements. Indexes can take up considerable space, however, so the analyst should take care that the index is really necessary.

8.3 | Access and security

In more complex systems with a number of users having access to the system, it may well be that users will only be able to access certain parts of the system. For example, when Freddo Smitho logs on to the system, we might allow him to order ingredients or add dishes, but we certainly would not want him dealing with the artistes, particularly Sharon Twain. As a result, we would need to design the interface available to each category of user. In large systems there might be many different categories of user, each with a different view of the system. The different views will need to be specified through separate interface design diagrams. These different views will then need to be built into the physical design of the system.

This is normally achieved by using the DBMS security features such as privileges and views. Privileges allow categories of users to perform certain operations. Users might be allowed to read or query information in a table, but not be allowed to update or delete information. It is common sense not to allow users access to more information than they need. Similarly, only a very few users should be allowed to update or delete information.

8.4 Volumetrics

As mentioned above, before we can make final decisions on hardware and storage requirements, we need to have some idea of the volume of data likely to be generated by our system. The likely volumes can be modelled using the entities on the entity model. The average number of occurrences of each entity is marked inside the entity box. So, if we have 15,000 patients in our system, we will write 15000 inside the PATIENT box. On average, each patient might have had two referrals, so we write 2 on the relationship with REFERRAL. This gives us 15,000 × 2 referrals on average, so we would write 30000 in the REFERRAL entity box. Figure 8.2 shows a model for the Medical Centre.

This diagram shows us the average number of occurrences for each entity during a specific time period. The time period is the life of the entity before it is deleted or archived. This will be determined by the Database Administrator and will vary from entity to entity. For example, we would expect to keep the patient information for many years before archiving or deleting. However, the work rota information will quickly become obsolete and can be deleted soon after the work has been done.

Figure 8.2 only estimates the number of records we can expect in a table at any one time; it does not tell us the size of each record. In order to acquire that information, we need to consider the size of each field in the table and expand our calculations accordingly. Figure 8.3 shows part of a spreadsheet which might be used to make the final calculations. This will give us a logical volumetric size of the database. In practice, databases are usually larger than the predicted size.

Note that the 'Size' data is taken from the format of the fields and the 'Volume' data is taken from the volumetrics diagram (Figure 8.2). The two tables, PATIENT and TREATMENT, will generate around 30 Mbyte of data in this example. A figure for all the entities in the system will be required and this will give us a good idea as to whether our planned hardware will be able to cope with the storage requirements.

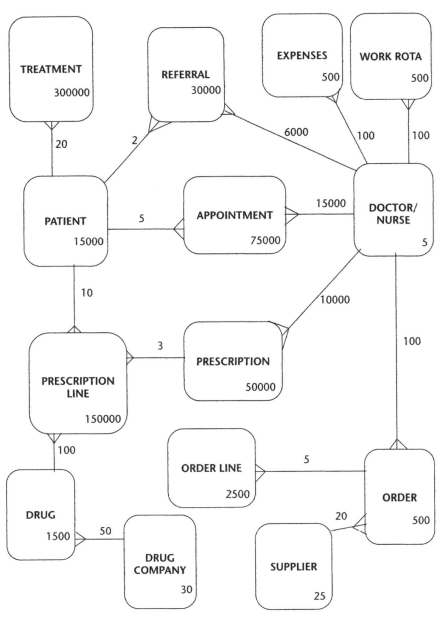

Figure 8.2
Volumetrics diagram.

8.5 Documentation

This is an area which tends to get ignored by many analysts. Having laboured over the analysis and design and having produced the perfect blueprint for the perfect system, the last thing anyone feels like doing is writing up the documentation. However, the documentation is the user's number one support tool. As a minimum, it should consist of:

Figure 8.3
Spreadsheet showing volumetric data for two tables.

PATIENT	Type	Size	Volume	Total (k)
PatientNo	Number	6	15000	90
P_FirstName	Text	15	15000	225
P_Surname	Text	20	15000	300
P_Address	Text	50	15000	750
P_TelHome	Text	15	15000	225
P_Mobile	Text	15	15000	225
P_Type	Text	5	15000	75
P_DateOfBirth	Date	8	15000	120
TREATMENT				
RecordNo	Number	8	300000	2400
PatientNo	Number	6	300000	1800
Date	Date	8	300000	2400
Condition	Text	20	300000	6000
PrescriptionNo	Number	10	300000	3000
Outcome	Text	40	300000	12000
			Grand Total =	**29520 kbyte**
			or	**29.5 Mbyte**

- a preliminary user guide
- a technical guide
- online help
- users may require a guide to the daily or weekly operations required

The user guide should be a clear set of instructions showing the user how to use the system. It must avoid technical language and jargon. It should be a training manual as well as a reference guide. Key sections will be the functions of the system and how to use the interface.

The online help should contain information about all the key procedures and components in the system. There could be information about the possible error messages and available reports and queries. This information should be indexed and also contain search facilities.

The technical guide should contain the data dictionary where all the data is defined; DFDs; entity models; system architecture information; and prototype information. This guide will be used primarily by the technical staff who will operate the system. In small organizations, there may not be any technical staff. In this case, the guide will have to be fairly general and may be included as a section in the user guide.

We are now in a position to hand over our designs to the programmer to develop and test the required code. Our job as a systems analyst is over and we would expect to see large amounts of money appearing imminently in our bank balance.

8.6 CASE tools

Computer-Assisted Systems Engineering (CASE) tools were originally developed in response to a number of problems experienced by systems analysts and their clients. Primarily, these problems can be summarized as: systems were expensive and didn't work. Apart from that, they were fine. It's not hard to see how the process of analysis and design can be tedious, slow and expensive. The phrase 'paralysis by analysis' is often used. CASE tools are an attempt to speed up the process and make it less prone to error.

CASE tools can be used to support many aspects of systems engineering. However, there are a large number of tools available which specifically support structured systems analysis and design techniques and methodologies.

CASE tools allow the analyst to draw DFDs and entity models which can be easily updated and amended as the need arises. This can save many hours of redrawing diagrams. They will also validate the diagrams to make sure that no errors of consistency have been made. For example, they will ensure that each DFD process box has at least one input and at least one output. Similarly, they will check that DFDs across different levels are consistent. As a result, CASE tools, once mastered, are likely to improve both the efficiency and the effectiveness of the analyst.

Many modern CASE tools will even generate required code from designs, particularly in the areas of prototyping, report generation and query design. The really good news is that they will generate reams of documentation too, but this comes with a serious health warning and will need careful editing.

Other features of CASE tools are:

● Support for reusable code

● Support for project groups

● Project management information and support

● Links to external products such as databases

● Pseudo-code generation

● Re-engineering of existing systems

There are four different types of CASE tool:

● Upper CASE
These are used in the strategic planning of information systems. They provide a structure for the planning phase of the systems life cycle.

● Middle CASE

These are used during the analysis and design phase of projects and tend to be the tools analysts mean when they refer to CASE tools.

● Lower CASE

These are used by programmers during the implementation and maintenance phases of projects to help develop and test code.

● Integrated CASE tools

These tools integrate the previous three into one tool. So they cover upper, middle and lower CASE tools.

It is worth bearing in mind that most time is expended on maintenance in the systems development life cycle. This is because new systems often have many errors or omissions which need correcting. This is classed as corrective maintenance.

Other types of maintenance might be adaptive maintenance, which requires changes to be made to allow the system to adapt to new technologies in the external environment; and perfective maintenance, which involves changing the system in response to changing user requirements. Maintenance can be very expensive, so it is important to try to minimize the need for it. This can only be done by careful and flexible design.

The use of CASE tools ought to pick up or eradicate many of these potential problems before the system is implemented. Analysts get tired, dispirited, bored, subversive and bad-tempered (often all at the same time), whereas CASE tools do not. They can automate much of the tedious stuff, leaving the analyst free to chew over that sticky design issue, or go for a game of golf.

Before one gets too carried away, it should not be forgotten that CASE tools do not guarantee a high-quality system. That remains the analyst's responsibility, and CASE tools will not put users at ease or tease out hidden requirements. They can be tricky to learn and use, but modern analysts will be expected to have one or two in their tool kit.

Summary

The system design is now complete. Some very general comments have been made about technical and physical design, but much will depend upon what hardware and software is chosen. It is now time to implement and test the system, but that is beyond the scope of this book.

Exercise

8.1 Design an interface for Freddo Smitho at Swillbuckets. He needs to be able to see and update information about dishes, ingredients, recipes and events. Use the entity model in Figure 6.4 to help you.

And finally...

Readers will be pleased to hear that Jack Trout is alive and well and has just opened the 'Cold Turkey Health Club' (Motto: 'Vim and Vigour') just down the road from Swillbuckets. Members can recharge their batteries while enjoying a relaxing massage from Phyllis Haddon. In this way, members pay him to make them ill at Swillbuckets and then pay him again to make them better at the health club. This is an iterative process.

Sadly, there is not such good news of the Medical Centre. A GPC investigation, prompted by an incorrect diagnosis of bubonic plague for a chickenpox sufferer, resulted in the discovery that Dr McLean was not a doctor after all. He just happened to possess a white coat and illegible handwriting. After being struck off, his last known whereabouts were as a consultant in a health club in West Yorkshire....

Teaching case study – North Sea Ferries

TITLE: NSF Project Information Document

Project Background

- North Sea Ferries is a small independent ferry operator.
- North Sea Ferries Head Office is at Hull.
- They have booking terminals at Hull, Amsterdam, Rotterdam and Zeebrugge.
- The company runs passenger and vehicle ferry services between Hull and the three other ports.
- The company owns four RORO (Roll On, Roll Off) ferries and one catamaran. Sometimes at busy times the company will charter other boats. The company may also have to do this if one of their own boats is being maintained or repaired.
- All crossings run on a regular timetable.
- Ferries usually carry a mixture of people on business, people on holiday and freight.
- At the moment the booking system is a manual one.
- Business has increased over the past few years, so the company feels it should start to use computerized systems.
- The company knows that most other ferry companies use computers.

- The company has problems with the system it is using now, and these problems will get worse as business increases.

Earlier this year, the company decided to have its existing systems for booking, issuing tickets and embarkation analysed. If this analysis is successful it could lead to the design and implementation of a computerized system.

Project Team – Terms of Reference

As a development team, your terms of reference are to:

- Carefully analyse the existing systems for booking, issuing tickets and embarkation control.

- Find out what the problems are at the moment with these systems.

- Find out what the new requirements are.

- Design a new system to meet the requirements.

Document this using Structured Systems Analysis and Design Method standards.

NSF Project Briefing Document

Company Overview – Crossing Bookings

NSF started off as a family firm. Many of the structures and procedures that the company has now have developed from this family origin.

The company has a number of separate functions involved with ferry bookings:

- The Central Booking Office at Hull deals with bookings and also with customer enquiries. So here staff deal with enquiries, reserve tickets for customers, make bookings for customers and provide general crossing information.

- The Crossing Desks are at the ports. Here, the staff deal with crossing queries, take last minute bookings, issue tickets, take cash payments and issue boarding passes.

- The Payment Control Department checks all payments and authorizes and issues tickets.

When bookings are made, all the details are recorded on a crossing booking form. This form is created at the desk where the booking is made. It is the main record of each booking.

The booking form is then sent from the desk where the booking is made, over to the central booking office. From the central booking office it is then sent to the payments control area for them to check the payment and issue the ticket. Finally, the form goes back to the central booking office where it is put in a file. The form is kept in the file for reference in the future and also to analyse places available on ferries.

Whenever a booking is made, the customers can pay by cash, credit card, or on account. If a customer has an account, they can put the amount on their account and they will receive an invoice later.

Some members of staff have been interviewed. Transcripts of these interviews are available.

Transcript of Interview with Booking Office Manager

The central booking office in Hull is open from 9 to 5, Monday to Friday. At all other times the answering machine is switched on. Bookings can be made on the answering machine and the details are confirmed with the customer later.

For normal crossings, customers can book 6 months ahead. The booking office has a record card for every crossing. All bookings are recorded on these cards.

The cards are stored in order so that the crossings that will be soonest are at the front of the drawer and the crossings that are a long time away are at the back. Sometimes two or more cards are stapled together if the crossings are very full and there is not enough space for all the information on one card.

Apart from the cards, every booking is also recorded on a booking form. These forms go to the Payments Control Department and also to Accounts. When they have been processed there, the forms come back to us in the booking office to be filed in the booking form archive file.

Most of our bookings are made by telephone. Some bookings are made by fax and a few are made by letter.

We have two sorts of customer. Some customers have an account – these customers get an invoice every month from the Accounts Department. Some customers do not have an account – they must pay before they get their tickets.

Some account customers (e.g. travel agents) may be booking through their account or they may be booking for one of their customers. It is very important to know who will be paying for the tickets, where the invoice should be sent and whose name should be on it. I will explain more about this later.

Telephone bookings here in the booking office can come from customers themselves and they can also come from the port desks. The procedure for both of these is almost the same, except that we have special members of staff who just deal with the port desks. If a booking is made outside office hours, the port desk writes out the details on a fax and send it to us. Every morning we use the faxes to make sure that our records are up to date. If a customer telephones us directly, the booking clerk has to find out which crossing they want. This means they need to know where the crossing goes from, where the crossing goes to, and the time and date of the crossing.

We only ever book single crossings. This means that a return is booked as a single there and a single back, each with a unique booking number. We then need to know who the customer is and what they require. We also need to include any vehicle details and whether they need a seat or a cabin.

If the booking is not going to go on a customer's account, we need to know who to send the invoice to and where to send it to. We need to know who the passengers are, and any special detail such as wheelchairs, medical problems or small babies. All these details are used to complete the booking form and to work out the total cost based on the booking tariff. If the customer later cancels the booking we change the details on the crossing record card for that ferry. We also fill in a booking cancellation form, which goes to Payment Control in the same way as a normal booking form.

Sometimes people telephone us and they want to travel very soon. This can mean that we do not have enough time to send them an invoice by post and receive the money from them. If this happens they can pay by credit card, by giving us the card number over the telephone. If this is not possible they can arrange to pay when they arrive to get on the ferry. These details must be written on the booking record card so that the desk staff will know what to do. They must also go on the booking form for Payments and Accounts.

If a person wants to pay by credit card we check their credit-worthiness (i.e. whether they are over the limit on their card). When we check this with the credit card company they give us an authorization number, which is then written on the booking form. We also go through the checking procedure if a person pays by credit card at the desk.

If a port desk phones us with a booking because they have a customer there who wants to make a booking, exactly the same procedure is followed. It is just as if the customer was phoning us. The only difference is that the desk staff can take the payment at the time and they can also give the customer the tickets. Account customers can of course also book at desks.

One problem we have with the booking system is when customers book by leaving the information on the answering machine. Quite often there is information missing.

When a booking is made out of hours (i.e. when the desk is shut) or when a desk takes money or issues tickets, they should fill in a booking form and then fax the form to us. Sometimes they forget to do this.

We keep a file of all account customers. We keep this file up to date from information we get from the Payments Control Department. This file contains a security procedure which people booking on behalf of this company must use. The procedure may involve using an order number, which must be quoted, or only certain people being allowed to make bookings.

When non-account customers receive an invoice, they should send the payment to the Accounts Department. The Accounts Department let the Payments Control people know that they can go ahead and issue the ticket. When the payment is made, Payment Control should tell us on the booking form so that we can keep our records up to date. Also, if tickets are issued at the desk, this information needs to be entered on the booking record so that the desks are aware of this. Often this information reaches us too late.

At the end of every day we fax copies of crossing record cards for the crossings on the next day to the desk at the port of departure. That desk then deals with last minute bookings and they also sell standby tickets. Standby tickets are slightly cheaper. They are available for all unbooked places, but they cannot be sold until 2 hours before departure.

Our biggest problems in here are that we receive vital information from Accounts very late. Also booking confirmation information is not clear and the answering machine is a problem. Everything else is fine. I suppose that the booking form could be designed better. There is loads of paperwork of course, but that's all part of working in an office.

Transcript of Interview with Port Desk Staff

We have a lot of problems here. What happens is that if a mistake is made somewhere else in the system, the passenger always ends up in here complaining.

I think we do three things that will be of interest to you. We act as go-betweens with the booking office if a passenger wants to make an advance booking. This means that we relay information that the booking office wants and also sometimes take the customer's payment. We also deal with checking in, boarding passes and last-minute bookings.

When the booking office closes it faxes copies of the crossing record cards to us. The cards give us all the information about latest bookings and passenger information. When the booking office is closed we can take bookings for crossings that will soon be departing. Sometimes the copies of the record cards are very messy and difficult to read. Usually the worst cards are the ones for the busiest crossings. We are supposed to sort out how many places there are left on the boats and sell them. When we do sell them, we have to fill in a booking form and fax it back to the booking office. If the customer wants the tickets on account, we have to check with the booking office that this is all right.

Sometimes passengers collect their tickets at check-in and sometimes they have to pay for them as well. Passengers can pay by cash or credit card. We are supposed to work all this out from the messy copies of the booking cards. At the end of every day we put the money in the bank, which has a branch on the port. When the bank gives us the paying-in slip, we send this to the sales ledger department in Accounts.

Two hours before the ferry goes, we can sell any leftover tickets or any reserved tickets that have not been paid for. It is very difficult for us to work out how many we have available to sell from the information on the crossing record cards. If we make a mistake the passengers get very angry when they realize that we have sold their seats to another passenger.

We have quite a few problems, as I have said. The worst one is working out what the crossing record card means. We can never even be sure that the information is up to date and correct. It is very embarrassing to be asking for money from a passenger who has already paid.

Another problem is that it is very difficult to cope when the booking office is closed. We use the latest crossing record cards, but sometimes we might make a booking for a ferry which is already full. Also, if the central booking office is closed we have no way of checking whether a customer can pay on account for crossings which are departing very soon.

Normally we only take account bookings from 9 to 5, but sometimes we have to make a decision ourselves. We really need a copy of the account customer file here and at every other desk.

When we take a booking or if we sell tickets, we fill in a booking form which is sent by fax to the central booking office. Sometimes, if we are very busy, it is difficult to do this properly. If we can't find and fill in the paperwork quickly enough the crossing can't be delayed. If the customer has paid there and then and the ship is about to leave; why does the booking office need to know anyway?

Could you change things so that we don't have to fill in all the unnecessary details on the booking forms? It would make our jobs much easier. Also, if you can persuade the booking office to let us have complete, correct information which is easy to read on the crossing records, then staff who have to deal with the public would find life a lot easier.

Examples of Documents used by North Sea Ferries

The following are examples of documents that the NSF use now. These were collected when the work areas of NSF were being researched. The documents are:

- Crossing Booking Form
- Booking Cancellation Form
- Crossing Record Card
- Load Factor Report
- Weekly Traffic Report
- Sample of Crossing Ticket
- Invoice
- Boarding Card

Crossing Booking Form		Booking Date:	Booking Number:	
Crossing Date:	Departure Time:		Arrival Time:	
Crossing Number:	Departure Port:		Arrival Port:	
Customer Name:			Seats Booked:	Cabins Booked:
Vehicle Details – Make and Model:			Reg. No:	

Passengers	Cabin	Seat	Special Requirements

Payment Name and Address:

Amount Due:	Payment Mode:
Account Number:	Invoice Number:
Date Charged:	Date Paid:
Credit Card Details:	Cash Payment Date:
Date Charged:	Received By:
Date of Ticket Issue:	

Booking Cancellation Form:	Cancellation Date:		Booking Number:
Crossing Date:	Departure Time:		Arrival Time:
Crossing Number:	Departure Port:		Arrival Port:
Passenger Name(s):			<u>Cabins Booked</u> <u>Seats Booked</u>
Payment Name and Address:			
Actioned By:			Action Date:

Crossing Record Card	Date:	
Crossing Date:	Departure Time:	Arrival Time:
Crossing Number:	Departure Port:	Arrival Port:
Vehicle Allocated:		Seats Available: Cabins Available:
Deck Crew:		Amenities Crew:

Passenger Name	Booking Date	Booking Status	Spec. Req.	Seat Booked	Cabin Booked

Load Factor Report

Date:

Crossing Number	Departure Time	Arrival Time	Vessel Type	Seats/ Cabins Available	Seats/Cabins Booked			%
					Firm	Reserved	Total	

Weekly Traffic Report

Date:

Departure Port	Arrival Port	No. of Crossings	No. of Passengers	% loading

---

North Sea Ferries   *passenger ticket*

Passenger Name:

Crossing No:	**Date:**	**Time:**

Seat/Cabin Type:

From: **To:**

Arrival time:

You will be given your seat/cabin number at the port.

Please check in one hour before departure.

                                        Booking Clerk:

North Sea Ferries

invoice

Invoice no:

Customer Name:

Crossing No:	No. passengers:	Price:	Total:
			Total due:

Please send payment with this invoice to:

North Sea Ferries, 25 Cross Street, Hull

Date paid: Accounts Clerk:

North Sea Ferries   *Boarding Card*

Passenger Name:

Crossing No: **Date:**   **Time:**

Seat/Cabin Number:

Bibliography

Connolly, T. and Begg, C. (1999). *Database Systems,* 2nd edn. Reading, MA: Addison-Wesley.

Fournier, R. (1999). *A Methodology for Client/Server and Web Application Development.* Upper Saddle River, NJ: Prentice Hall.

Goodland, M. with Slater, S. (1995). *SSADM A Practical Approach.* New York: McGraw-Hill.

Hoffer, J. A., George, J. F. and Valacich, J. S. (1998). *Modern Systems Analysis and Design,* 2nd edn. Reading, MA: Addison-Wesley.

Weaver, P. L., Lambrou, N. and Walkley, M. (1998). *Practical SSADM,* 2nd edn. London: Financial Times Professional.

Index

04-03 15:24 Job: 28054-1-9780333986301 28054-B356D-1T TPS: 254x178 T:225 inkjetC

CPI Antony Rowe
Eastbourne, UK
April 03, 2019